Useful Trees

For Homesteading & Self-Reliance

Nathan Dickeson

ISBN: 9798300727710

DEDICATION

To all the friends who made finishing this book possible.

CONTENTS

AUTHORS NOTE

I have a few things I'd like to mention.

1. I hope you'll find some trees that will be useful for your homestead. I tried to include as many useful trees as I could think of, but obviously there are many trees I will have missed. So, if your favorite tree isn't here, please reach out to me.

2. Even though it's a common practice for this type of book, you'll notice that there are no grainy black and white pictures. I think it's a waste of effort and ink. To make my point, look up a redbud tree and tell me a black and white picture would have done it justice. If you want to know what a tree looks like, just google it. This will also keep printing costs low, so I can charge less.

3. Let's talk "invasives." The very first tree in this book is the black locust. This is an incredibly useful tree native to my region, but every time I talk about it, someone on the internet yells at me for promoting an invasive plant. So, here's the deal. I'll tell you about the different uses that a tree has, and if it's highly invasive in your area, it's your job to use your best judgment on if you should utilize it or not.

CHAPTER 1
MY FAVORITE TREES

This chapter is pretty self-explanatory. It has my top ten favorite trees. I have more than just 10 favorites, but those stayed within their respective chapters. These ten trees aren't even necessarily the best at their specific task... that said, for the most part, they are the best.

Black Locust

The black locust is my favorite tree. It grows incredibly fast, the wood doesn't rot, and the flowers are beautiful, but that's not all. This tree has so many uses. However, because this tree is so incredible, it has nasty thorns to protect itself, which gives it a bad name.

In the spring it creates these impressive bunches of flowers. The flowers are edible and very popular amongst foragers, and the nectar from those flowers makes a premium honey called Acacia Honey. However, when those flowers mature into bean pods, the beans are toxic. The leaves are an excellent feed source for animals, with a similar nutritional profile to alfalfa, which is why a nickname for it is Tree Alfalfa. That said, if you try to feed your livestock nothing but black locust, it will make them sick.

In the fall, the leaves turn a brilliant golden color, and the bean pods fall to the ground. The wood is also incredible. It doesn't rot, and because of this, the original homesteaders grew these trees so that they could have fence posts that would never decay. It's also a high BTU wood. It is considered one of the best firewoods on the planet, but be careful. It burns so hot it can ruin your stove.

This tree is one of the best nitrogen fixers and it grows very fast. That makes this an excellent choice for coppicing. This can be for firewood, fence posts, etc. However, when you do cut this tree, it'll create suckers. This can be a good thing or a bad thing, depending on how you look at it. To me, that means I get free voluntary trees. To someone else, that means they have to come back and kill the new saplings. Now, the main reason you should plant black locust is because of its incredible nitrogen fixing capabilities. Plant this tree right next to your fruit, and other useful trees. At the beginning of each year, coppice the black locust. When you coppice a tree, the roots die back, and in this case, release nitrogen into the soil, fertilizing the plants around it. This will boost the growth of your fruit tree, and over the course of the year, the black locust will come back with a vengeance, just in time for you to coppice it again.

Medicinally it's been used for many different things but primarily the root bark has a numbing effect, which is good for toothaches. The dried leaves are used for burns.

Latin: Robinia pseudoacacia
Grow Zone: 3-7
Ornamental: Yes
Medicinal: Yes
Growth Rate: 4ft+
Animal feed: Yes
Wood: Burning, doesn't rot, fence posts
Height: 40-60ft
Coppicing: Yes
Nitrogen Fixer: Yes

PROs
The best nitrogen fixer
Wood doesn't rot
One of the best firewoods
Beautiful spring and Fall colors
Excellent honey
Fast growing
Leaves are a good animal feed

CONs
Thorns
Seeds are toxic
Suckers

Empress Paulownia

Paulownia is my second favorite tree. This tree has gorgeous purple flowers in the spring that the bees love. However, the reason why this tree is so incredible is because it's one of the fastest growing trees in the world. It grows up to ten feet per year and is ready to cut for timber in just ten years. It also does great at being coppiced, which means you can regrow it for timber from the already existing roots.

The leaves are awesome too. They're massive and full of nitrogen, making them perfect for compost, green fertilizer, or for chop and drop. These leaves are also high in protein, perfect for feeding your animals.

Don't plant near a house. This tree gets big fast, and the branches have a nasty habit of falling in heavy winds. The roots are good at destroying foundations.

The tree is not considered a great medicinal plant but it has a history of being used to treat many different issues, including asthma, ulcers, bronchitis, and many other ailments.

Latin: Paulownia tomentosa
Grow Zone: 7-10
Ornamental: Yes
Medicinal: Maybe
Growth Rate: 10ft+
Animal Feed: Yes
Wood: Timber
Height: 30-70ft
Coppicing: Yes
Nitrogen Fixer: Yes

PROs
Fast growth
Flowers
Animal feed
Nitrogen fixer
Green fertilizer
Light weight & strong wood

CONs
Brittle branches
Aggressive roots
Wood is soft and easily scratched

Mulberry

My 3rd favorite tree is the mighty mulberry. This tree isn't a nitrogen fixer, but it still grows incredibly fast. Part of this is due to its abundance of nutritious leaves, and part of it is due to all the birds that love its berries, who then make manure deposits all around it. Those birds aren't the only ones who can benefit from eating those leaves and berries. Yes, you can enjoy them too. It's a commonly consumed leafy green. However, this tree can be one of your best sources for animal feed. The leaves are full of nutrients and lots of protein.

The berries are awesome too. Think blackberry, but on a tree, and not on a little thorny bush. Here's the thing, you will never be able to pick them all, so it's a good idea to give your chickens access to the base of the tree. They'll enjoy the berries that fall to the ground, and they'll enjoy the bugs who will try to enjoy the berries, but instead become chicken food.

The wood is incredibly versatile. It's popular for woodworking. It's a great smoking wood. It is decently rot resistant. Lastly, it is a great firewood. It is one of the highest BTU woods and burns nicely. This tree is also good at being coppiced.

The red mulberry is native to the USA and the white mulberry is considered invasive in some locations, but if you're interested in silkworms, the white mulberry is their only feed source. They can eat other mulberry leaves, but white is what they like.

Medicinal uses include using the bark for stomach aches, leaves and twigs for colds, sore throat, coughs, insect bites and wounds. They also apparently help stabilize blood sugar levels, helping with diabetics.

Warning, the male mulberry tree is a nightmare for allergies and doesn't produce any fruit. Males are not needed for the female to produce fruit. If you have any males, you can coppice them and use them as animal feed, just don't let them grow big and produce pollen.

Latin: Morus
Grow Zone: 5-10
Ornamental: No
Medicinal: Yes
Growth Rate: 5ft+
Animal Feed: Yes
Wood: Lots of uses
Height: 70-80ft
Coppicing: Yes
Nitrogen Fixer: No

PROs
Fruit
Quality wood
Smoking meat
Firewood
Mulch/green fertilizer
Animal feed

CONs
Bird poop
Insects, if berries are left to rot
Allergies

Black Walnut

Black walnut is America's favorite wood. It's beautiful, and due to demand, expensive. Black walnut syrup is also popular. Yes, you can tap a black walnut, just like a maple tree. Compared to English walnuts, the nuts suck. They are the hardest nut to crack, and they tend to crumble. The flavor isn't commonly thought of as good either. Some say it's even more bitter than the English walnut, but as for my experience with them, I'd say they taste like soap. However, apparently some people think the black walnuts flavor is far superior. That said, if you train your pigs to eat them, it's an excellent feed source. The husk of the nuts can also be used as a dye.

So, to sum up, you have a tree that provides you with nuts, syrup, and in 30 years when you want to retire, a very profitable wood.

One word of caution, black walnuts don't like competition, so they exude a chemical called juglone to kill off any plants that can't handle it. You'll have to look up lists of juglone tolerant plants, but in general, plants native to North America can handle it better than foreign plants.

Latin: Juglans nigra
Grow Zone: 4-9
Ornamental: No
Medicinal: No
Growth Rate: 2-3ft
Animal Feed: Nuts
Wood: Premium
Height: 70-90
Coppicing: Yes
Nitrogen Fixer: No

PROs
Premium wood
Syrup
Nuts

CONs
Juglone

Willow

The willow tree, particularly the weeping willow, is an iconic tree, but did you know willows are also a useful tree? The bark of willow limbs can replace your aspirin. The bark contains a chemical called salicin, which is the main chemical required for making aspirin.

Now let's talk leaves. If you soak the leaves in water, you can use that water as a rooting hormone, which is used to make your cuttings have a better success rate. The leaves themselves can be used to make rope or they can be used as a great animal feed.

Willows grow fast, so it's a good source of "okay" firewood, but if you turn that wood into charcoal, willow charcoal is considered The Premium Charcoal. That's not the only use for willow wood. If you want to weave baskets or weave structures for your garden, the young willow branches are one of the top weaving limbs. Young willow limbs are very flexible and again, willow grows very fast, so you can produce a lot.

The cool thing about willow is that its roots can handle a lot of water, meaning it's a tree that can be planted in a swampy area or along creek banks. Those same roots are good at filtering and purifying that water and they will also protect that same bank from erosion and flooding.

Depending on the variety of willows, it can grow from a cold climate to a subtropical climate.

Latin: Salix
Grow Zone: 3-10
Ornamental: No
Medicinal: Yes
Growth Rate: 4ft+
Animal Feed: Yes
Wood: Charcoal
Height: 40-80ft
Coppicing: Yes
Nitrogen Fixer: No

PROs
Fast growing
Pain killer
Rooting hormone
Animal feed
Weaving
Rope
Water filtering
Prevents soil erosion
Charcoal
Firewood

CONs
Can be trashy

Sea Berry

Also known as sea buckthorn, this isn't actually a tree, it's a large shrub, but a few shrubs are going to sneak their way into this book, and this one is so cool it made it onto my favorites list.

Citrus is a tropical fruit, so if you live somewhere where it snows, you can't grow citrus without a greenhouse. But here's the thing, humanity loves citrus, so we import it. Sea berry is not citrus, but it is a little orange fruit that tastes citrusy. Think sour like a lemon, but with orange notes. It's popular in drinks and for flavoring things like ice cream. Like citrus, it is high in vitamin-c, but unlike citrus, its fruit is a creamy fruit, full of fats. Examples of fatty fruits are avocados & olives.

This fruit being full of fats means you can use it to make oil, and sea berry oil has been used medicinally in the Himalayas since ancient times. Its predominant medicinal uses are for healing or improving skin & hair related problems. Dryness, scars, thinning, etc. Nutritionally it is an omega and vitamin-c powerhouse. Oh, and speaking of the Himalayas, they're cold, aren't they? Unlike citrus, the sea berry bush can withstand the coldest environments humans like to live in.

This plant is also a nitrogen fixer, which is always a plus, and as you might've guessed from its name, it's capable of salty environments, which is rare. However, this thing is thorny. There's a reason why it's called sea buckthorn. One last note, it hates the shade, with a passion. It needs sun.

Latin: Hippophae rhamnoides
Grow Zone: 2-7
Ornamental: No
Medicinal: Yes
Fruiting rate: 3-4 Years
Animal Feed: Yes
Wood: No
Height: 18ft
Coppicing: Yes
Nitrogen Fixer: Yes

PROs
Fruit
Nitrogen fixer

CONs
Thorns
Needs full sun

Redbud

Redbud is probably the least useful tree in this chapter. It made it on here solely because it's such a beautiful tree. It is one of the earliest bloomers. As soon as winter ends this tree gives you beautiful pink petals, while everything else still looks dead.

However, that doesn't mean this isn't an incredibly useful tree. Those petals, they're edible, and are often used to make jelly or to flavor sodas. This tree is part of the pea family so when those petals mature, they form little pea pods, which you or your animals can eat. Don't forget, peas are full of protein, so just like peas, the redbud pods are a useful feed additive.

Supposedly it's also called the spice tree, because its bark is used to season meats. I said supposedly, because I was unable to find any real examples of someone doing this. However, it is a great wood for smoking meat.

Medicinally the bark is used to treat whooping cough, and the inner bark and roots are used to treat congestion, fevers, and vomiting.

This is a faster growing tree, but it's surprisingly slow for being a nitrogen fixer. This means, while yes, it is a nitrogen fixer, it's not a good one.

Redbuds are also an understory tree, so they can handle shade better than most and are typically a smaller tree. This, plus how beautiful its flowers are, makes it a popular ornamental tree.

Latin: Cercis canadensis
Grow Zone: 4-9
Ornamental: Yes
Medicinal: Yes
Growth Rate: 2ft+
Animal Feed: Yes
Wood: Beautiful
Height: 20-30
Coppicing: No
Nitrogen Fixer: Yes

PROs
Beautiful
Tasty petals
Smoking wood
Pea protein feed

CONs
Not the best nitrogen fixer

American Chestnut

The American chestnut, an environmental tragedy. Now the environmentalists don't like me much. However, one thing we can all agree on is the tragedy of the American chestnut. Imagine if the redwood trees in California all just died. That's what happened in the east. The eastern forests of America used to be filled with American chestnuts. One out of every four trees were chestnut trees, & these trees were massive. Again, compare it to the giant redwoods. American chestnuts were the towering giants of the east. A little over a hundred years ago, the trees got infected with a blight & they all died. There are a few trees left, but the American chestnut is functionally extinct... or is it?

Ever since the American chestnut was all but wiped out, organizations have been breeding the survivors to try and make a blight resistant cultivar of the American chestnut, and it's getting close. Recently, there have also been organizations trying to make a GMO variety that is immune to the blight. In general, I'm wary of GMOs but with this tree I'd make an exception.

Chestnuts are a global favorite & are good eaten raw or roasted. Americans lost that part of our culture when our chestnut was wiped out, but you can still hear it in our Christmas songs.

If you're interested in just the nuts, there are European, Chinese, & Japanese Chestnuts, all of which produce great nuts. All chestnuts produce a ton of nuts every year & start producing within a few years.

American chestnuts were a special timber tree, praised to be one of the best woods for every application. Its rot resistance, strength, & ease of workability made it the premier wood.

As of the writing of this book you can technically get American chestnut seeds that have a good chance of being resistant to the blight. Their parents are, but that's not a guarantee. Those seeds are also expensive. However, if everything goes according to different chestnut organizations plans, blight resistant American chestnuts, available in mass, are only a few years away. We're getting so close.

Latin: Castanea dentata
Grow Zone: 4-8
Ornamental: No
Medicinal: Yes
Growth Rate: 5+
Animal Feed: Yes
Wood: Great
Height: 100ft+
Coppicing: Yes
Nitrogen Fixer: No

PROs
Nuts
Great wood
Rot resistant wood

CONs
Semi-extinct

Mimosa

The mimosa tree, also known as the Persian silk tree, or the happiness tree. Its Latin name is Albizia julibrissin. I am not talking about Mimosa tenuiflora/hostilis. That is a completely different plant and is popular amongst druggies.

The mimosa tree is a popular ornamental tree. When I was in St. George, it was planted everywhere. It produces a ton of beautiful & unique looking flowers. Hummingbirds love those flowers, but you'll love them too. Those flowers are used to make an herbal tea that is one of nature's top mood boosters, and the bark is one of the best antidepressants.

The mimosa is also one of the top nitrogen fixers. From what I can tell, nothing beats black locust besides maybe alder. However, the mimosa is still very good and unlike the black locust, it doesn't have thorns. I'll be using both. It just depends on the location.

Latin: Albizia julibrissin
Grow Zone: 6-9
Ornamental: Yes
Medicinal: Yes
Growth Rate: 3ft+
Animal Feed: Yes
Wood: Firewood
Height: 20-40ft
Coppicing: Yes
Nitrogen Fixer: Yes

PROs
Great nitrogen fixer
Herbal medicine
Flowers for pollinators

CONs
Messy

Red Maple

Red maples are better than sugar maples. I said it, I meant it. You can still make maple syrup from red maples; it just takes a larger amount of sap. In every other aspect, the red maple is better. It handles the shade better. It grows faster. Its fall colors are vibrant red, hence the name. It's less picky about soil. It's less picky about water. It's less susceptible to disease.

Sugar maples can handle the extreme cold better & live a long time. If you already have a mature sugar maple, that's awesome! If you're planting a maple tree, & are hoping to have a mature tree fast, plant red maple.

Maple wood is popular for woodworking and for smoking. The red maple is most often planted for its beautiful fall colors. It's still a slow growing tree, just like all maples, but it grows a lot faster than the rest.

Latin: Acer rubrum
Grow Zone: 4-9
Ornamental: Yes
Medicinal: No
Growth Rate: 2ft+
Animal Feed: No
Wood: Good
Height: 40-60ft
Coppicing: No
Nitrogen Fixer: No

PROs
Syrup
Fall colors

CONs
Maples are slow growers

CHAPTER 2
FRUIT TREES

In this chapter we will cover several useful fruit trees. In the last chapter we already talked about two fruit trees. You can go read about seaberries and mulberries in the previous chapter. The first half of this chapter will cover the most popular fruits that grow in temperate climates. The second half will cover incredible temperate fruits that aren't sold in the grocery stores, but you as a homesteader should totally consider growing. Now, most temperate fruits will grow in cold regions, and I'll cover heat loving fruits like citrus in a later chapter.

Apple

Apples are the most iconic fruit in the world. There are thousands of varieties. They've been bred to grow in cold regions like Alaska, and hot dry regions like Arizona. You can't go too hot, they still need a cold season, but Arizona is still pretty hot. If you've ever bought apples, you'll know that they are one of the most shelf stable fruits. Historically apples, when stored in a root cellar, is how people had fresh fruit in the winter. Remember, canning is a relatively new technology.

That said, sweet tasting apples are relatively new too. The main use of apples was to turn them into hard cider, also known as alcohol, and to make apple cider vinegar. Alcohol and vinegar have countless uses around the homestead but I'll let you look that up yourself.

Apple worms can become a big problem but they can be minimized by selecting resilient varieties, and by keeping the ground clear of rotting apples. Chickens and pigs are also useful in disrupting the life cycle of those little pests. Let them have access to your orchard in the early fall. The infected apples are the first to fall.

Latin: Malus domestica
Grow Zone: 3-8
Uses: Cider
Growth Rate: 2-3ft
Season: Early Fall
Height: 30ft
Fruit: 4 Years

PROs
Shelf stable

CONs
Worms

Pear

Pears are cool. Pears are one of the top crops for calories produced per acre. Pears, corn, and potatoes all produce a ton of calories in a small space. Pear juice is also the number one fruit juice drunk in the world. Not because it's the tastiest, but because it's the best at absorbing the flavors of other juices. It's also really easy to produce in large quantities.

My parents had pear trees and they never once did anything to take care of them. They've never been pruned, fertilized, or watered. Each summer we pick some of the fruit, and that's it. That won't always be the case, especially as you go into dry cold regions, but it generally is an easy tree. Each year we simply harvested the pears and forgot about the trees until next year.

Pears are one of the best fruits for drying and for canning. They're easy to process and taste great. I don't even like fresh pears, but dried pears are a great snack, and canned pears are delicious.

Latin: Pyrus communis
Grow Zone: 4-10
Uses: Juice
Growth Rate: 2ft
Season: Late Summer
Height: 20ft
Fruit: 4 Years

PROs
Calories
Juice
Snacks

CONs
I dislike them fresh

Asian Pear

Asian pears are different from pears but only slightly. They taste just like pears but are shaped more like apples and have a firmer texture like apples. Everything I just talked about with pears holds true for Asian pears, but there's two things to mention about Asian pears. Unlike European pears, Asian pears contain a special enzyme in them that is excellent at tenderizing meat. Asian pears are unfortunately easily bruised, so you have to be careful when harvesting. Pears you can just chuck in a bucket. Asian pears, if you ever see them in a store, have a protective foam net on them to protect them.

Latin: Pyrus pyrifolia
Grow Zone: 5-9
Uses: Meat
Growth Rate: 2ft
Season: Late Summer
Height: 30ft
Fruit: 4 Years

PROs
Tenderizes meat

CONs
Easily bruised

Quince

It looks like a pear, but it's super dense. Think of quince like cutting into a raw potato. This is a fruit you bake. You can eat it raw, but it's not something most people would enjoy. The way it's most often consumed is as a jam, and this is why it's useful. Quince is an extremely high pectin fruit. With modern industry you can buy pectin derived from citrus peels, but historically how most people got the pectin needed for making jams and preserves was through this fruit. The skin and the cores can be used to provide pectin for other low pectin fruits like most berries.

It's also an incredibly fragrant fruit. People use it to scent their homes. Bugs and other pests usually will leave the fruit alone, even when ripe and on the ground. The tree is a tough tree. It handles drought and cold very well, and it doesn't require much maintenance.

Latin: Cydonia oblonga
Grow Zone: 5-9
Uses: Pectin
Growth Rate: 2ft+
Season: Late Summer
Height: 15ft
Fruit: 5 Years

PROs
Provides pectin

CONs
Gross raw

Pomegranate

Pomegranates are an incredible fruit—one of my favorites—but if you've never had one, it can look a little different. Unlike most fruits, the seeds are what you eat. Recently, pomegranate juice is becoming a popular drink. Pomegranates have a sweet, sour flavor, and they are my family's special Christmas treat. It makes a mess to eat, but it's worth it.

Pomegranates are another one of your winter fresh fruit options. Nothing beats apples in longevity, but pomegranates will last for a couple months in the fridge, and like apples have a late season.

If you're far enough south for pomegranates but just barely too far north for citrus, pomegranate makes a decent substitute for a nice citrus like source for vitamin-C.

Latin: Punica granatum
Grow Zone: 6-10
Uses: Winter Fruit
Growth Rate: 1-2ft
Season: Late Fall
Height: 12ft
Fruit: 3 Years

PROs
Delicious
Shelf life
Winter fruit

CONs
Messy fruit

Peach

Peaches are my favorite fruit. Unfortunately, their season is short, and their shelf life is pretty small. This is because they are full of sugar.

Like apples and pears, peaches produce a ton of calories in a small space. Not as many as pears, but still a large amount. The cool thing about peaches is, they're easy to grow from seed. Stone fruits like peaches, plums, and apricots have a large seed at the center, this is why they're called stone fruits. If you want a lot of trees, for cheap, plant the pits from the stone fruits you eat. Unlike apples, a peach grown from seed will taste very close to the peach it came from.

Now when you plant most fruit trees. It will take them several years to start producing fruit. This is true regardless of if you plant a sapling or plant a seed. We plant saplings for a guaranteed taste and to shorten this timeline by a couple years. The awesome thing about peaches is that a peach pit, planted, will start producing fruit in just 3 years.

Latin: Prunus persica
Grow Zone: 4-9
Uses: Food
Growth Rate: 2ft
Season: Mid-Summer
Height: 25ft
Fruit: 3 Years

PROs
Delicious

CONs
Short season

Nectarines

Nectarines are my favorite cousins of peaches. They are so closely related, I don't know why they're not just considered an early variety of peach. That's actually why I love nectarines. Peach season is too short and nectarine season is just before peach season. Nectarines have thinner, non-hairy skin, and the flesh is firmer, with a tangy note.

Latin: Prunus persica var. nucipersica.
Grow Zone: 5-9
Uses: Food
Growth Rate: 2ft
Season: Mid-Summer
Height: 25ft
Fruit: 4 Years

PROs
Firmer than peaches
Non-fuzzy skin
Slightly earlier season than peaches

CONs
Extra short season

Apricots

Apricots are a delicious fruit, both fresh and dried. Dried apricots are probably the most popular and the easiest fruit to dry, besides maybe grapes. You simply split it open and let the sun or a dehydrator do its thing. Apricots are fairly easy to grow but they like to flower early so if you get a late frost, you most likely won't have apricots that year.

The seeds of the apricot have been used medicinally to some degree, but primarily apricot seed oil is a common oil for cosmetic uses.

Latin: Prunus armeniaca
Grow Zone: 5-8
Uses: Dried, cosmetics
Growth Rate: 2ft
Season: Summer
Height: 25ft
Fruit: 4 Years

PROs
Drying

CONs
Susceptible to frost

Cherry

Cherries can be split into two groups. Sour cherries and sweet cherries. Sour cherries grow in zones 4-6. Sweet cherries grow in zones 5-7. Sour cherries are easier to grow, but as the name suggests, are sour. Sweet cherries are popular as a snacking fruit. Sour cherries are used in baked goods. Cherries, but especially sweet cherries, have a problem with late frosts. They flower early in the spring and can be damaged by the cold temperatures.

Latin: Prunus avium/cerasus
Grow Zone: 4-7
Uses: Treats
Growth Rate: 1ft
Season: Early Summer
Height: 30ft
Fruit: 5 Years

PROs
Snacks
Baked goods

CONs
Frost damage

Plum

Plums, like apples, come in many different varieties, but the ones in the grocery stores of America are typically just one type, so if you're like me and you don't like plums, you might try some of the other varieties. When dried, plums are called prunes, and like apricots, prune plums are super easy to dry. Prunes have been used to treat constipation and as a sweetener before sugar was common.

Oh, and speaking of apricots, plums and apricots are so closely related it's easy to cross breed them to create hybrids. For example, the pluot is primarily a plum, with some apricot characteristics and the aprium is primarily an apricot with some plum characteristics.

Asian plums bloom early and fruit early, and they are typically for making juices and wines. European plums show up to the scene later and are typically the ones dried into prunes and are used as a fruity sweetener. American hybrid plums are a combination of these two.

Plums, like most fruit trees, hate wet feet, but plums in particular, have a hard time with it. So, if you have heavy clay, they might be a challenge.

Latin: Prunus domestica
Grow Zone: 3-9
Uses: Dried, sweetener
Growth Rate: 1.5ft
Season: Summer
Height: 15ft
Fruit: 3-6 Years

PROs
Easy to harvest
Dried fruit
Juicing

CONs
Hates soggy environments

Saskatoon

Saskatoon, juneberry, serviceberry, and shadbush all are names for this fruit. Depending on the variety it can be a bush, or it can be a tree. Saskatoons are similar to blueberries, but they aren't picky about acidity, and they ripen sooner. They look similar to blueberries, but with a reddish tint. Flavor wise, think blueberry, and cherry, with an almond aftertaste. The cool thing about saskatoons is that they ripen early in the year. They ripen 45 60 days after flowering, a few weeks before blueberries. Oh, and those flowers? Gorgeous! Saskatoon flowers are early spring flowers and are frost resistant. The fall colors aren't too bad either. The leaves turn a bright red in the fall.

One of the reasons this plant has so many names is because it has many different varieties and is native to every state and province in North America. You can find it wild, but obviously you'll get better fruit if you go with a cultivated variety. America doesn't grow this as a commercial crop but Canada does. The saskatoon berries were used to make pemmican and the twigs and leaves have medicinal uses. The leaves are used for stomach issues and the bark and branches are used for post pregnancy and menstrual healing. By the way, don't just start eating branches because you read it in a book.

Latin: Amelanchier alnifolia
Grow Zone: 2-7
Uses: ornamental, fruit
Growth Rate: 1.5ft
Season: Early Summer
Height: 6-25ft
Fruit: 3-4 Years

PROs
Pretty flowers & fall color
Early berries
Bush or tree

Sumac

Speaking of a citrus substitute, let's talk about sumac. Sumacs, particularly staghorn, smooth and lemonade berry are all closely related & have one special use. Sumac is used to make a lemonade-like drink. If you live in a place where it snows, citrus has to be grown in a pot or a greenhouse. Sumac is what the tribes in North America used to make their zesty drink.

Up north, it was staghorn sumac. Down south, smooth sumac. Out west, lemonade berry. They all do the same thing. By soaking them in cold water that water gets that sour twang humans love for their drinks. Don't wash the berries beforehand. The sour flavor is contained as an outer coating on the fruit.

Sumac is also a popular spice, particularly in middle eastern cuisine. If you've ever had hummus, that red powder was probably sumac, and za'atar is a popular spice mix that contains sumac.

It's an ornamental shrub too. The leaves turn a brilliant red in the fall & the berries provide a source of food for animals in the winter. They're a dry berry, so they don't rot if left on the tree, like other berries. Yes, there is poison sumac. No, it doesn't look like the other sumacs. Poison sumac has white berries & likes shaded wetlands. The tasty sumacs are sun lovers with combs of red berries.

Latin: Rhus
Grow Zone: 3-8
Uses: Spice, lemonade
Growth Rate: 2ft
Season: Late Summer
Height: 30ft
Fruit: 4 years

PROs
Lemonade
Spice

CONs
Needs sun

Autumn Olive

The most important thing about this plant is its lycopene content. One of the main health benefits you get from eating tomatoes is their lycopene content. Lycopene fights free radicals, protecting you from cancer. Autumn olives have 17x the amount of lycopene content that tomatoes have. The fruit is a tart sweet fruit, great for snacking and great for jams. Lycopene is most bioavailable when cooked, so for the health benefits, jams are great.

It's not native, but you'll find autumn olives all over the USA. That's because this bush is incredible at soil rehabilitation and preventing erosion. So back during the great depression the government had them planted all along highways and mining operations. It being planted everywhere, having an abundance of berries that birds like, and not being native, makes this a hated plant in some circles and is banned in some states.

I'm quite fond of this shrub. Like I just stated, it's incredible at soil rehabilitation. It grows in crappy soil. It's also a nitrogen fixer, so it helps fertilize your other crops. It grows in heavy shade. It even handles severe drought. Even with no rain it'll still produce fruit. It grows fast and creates suckers, which you can then chop and use as fertilizer. So in other words, it's a great shrub to grow under your orchard. It will aid in the growth of your trees and provide a second crop in the same space.

This shrub is probably my most controversial tree in this chapter. It's classified as an invasive in many states. It grows fast and can be hard to manage. But what makes certain people hate it is the fact that it has plenty of nasty thorns to remind you of its presence.

Latin: Elaeagnus umbellata
Grow Zone: 3-8
Uses: Nitrogen
Growth Rate: 2ft
Season: Early Fall
Height: 14ft
Fruit: 2-3 years

PROs
Fruit
Nitrogen fixing
Shade tolerant
Drought tolerant

CONs
Thorns
Illegal in some states

Persimmon

Persimmons are an orange colored, apricot to apple sized fruit that are especially popular in Asian countries. A good nickname for this fruit would be the squishy fruit. This fruit is unique because you don't typically eat them when they're firm like an apple, you wait till they're mushy & gooey. American persimmons, you literally can't eat until they are gooey. They're astringent, meaning full of tannins that will make your mouth go dry, and it won't taste good. However, with Asian persimmons, the majority are still astringent, but there are two types you can eat when they're firm. It's still popular to wait till they soften, cause the older the persimmon is, the sweeter it is.

Speaking of, old, dried persimmons are like jelly candies. So, eat them fresh, let them age, or let them dry. Your choice.

American persimmons are smaller & grow in zones 4-9. You cannot eat those fresh, they must be squishy. Asian persimmons grow in zones 7-11. Some Asian varieties can be eaten when firm.

I've only ever had one persimmon and I didn't like it all that much, it has a strong mushy pumpkin taste, but there's many different varieties and lots of people love them.

Latin: Diospyros kaki/virginiana
Grow Zone: 4-11
Uses: snacking
Growth Rate: 1.5ft
Season: Late Fall
Height: 60ft
Fruit: 3-6 Years

PROs
Can be dried into a candy

CONs
Not all are edible when firm

Pawpaw

Have you ever wanted that tropical taste but live somewhere that is definitely not tropical? The pawpaw is a tree native to the eastern half of North America.

The flavor is tropical but can be wildly different depending on your specific tree. Some taste like mango, others like bananas. Papia, pineapple, and cantaloupe, have all been used to describe its taste. The fruit has a creamy texture like an avocado or mango & is shaped like a green potato. However, it will never be in a grocery store. It has a very short shelf life of only a couple of days. So, enjoy them while you can.

This fruit has one major drawback. The seeds are highly toxic. If your pigs and chickens get access to your pawpaw tree, they could die. There's plenty of trees with toxic seeds, but usually either the animals avoid them, or only are toxic in large amounts. So, while some might say something is toxic, it's not a big deal. Pawpaw can kill your animals if you're not careful.

Latin: Asimina triloba
Grow Zone: 5-8
Uses: tropical fruit
Growth Rate: 1-2ft
Season: Late Summer
Height: 30ft
Fruit: 4 years

PROs
Tropical tasting fruit

CONs
Poisonous seeds
No shelf life

Jujube

Think of this as a super sweet mild green apple. It is described as an apple mixed with honey. Also known as the Chinese date, jujube popular in other parts of the world and can be eaten in all sorts of different stages. When young and underripe, it has more of a tart flavor, similar to a sour apple. When it's mature, it has a mild apple taste that is extra sweet. When old and dried out, they taste similar to dates. Medicinally jujube is supposed to help with anxiety.

Now the cool thing about jujube is that it can grow in decently cold places, to pretty hot locations. It really does like hot summers, but it can be grown in cold regions. That said, it's the Chinese jujube can be grown in colder climates. There is a cousin that is so closely related to the Chinese jujube, that even experts confuse the two. The Thai/Indian jujube tree grows in the tropics. So, effectively the jujube can grow in most locations across the globe.

Latin: Ziziphus jujuba
Grow Zone: 6-9
Uses: Anxiety
Growth Rate: 2ft+
Season: Early Fall
Height: 50ft
Fruit: 3 years

PROs
Ripens at different times
Can be harvested at different stages.

CONs
Thorns

CHAPTER 3
NUT TREES

Fun fact about nuts. Nut trees are fruit trees. Almost all nuts are just the tasty seeds contained in an inedible fruit. Don't believe me? Almonds and apricots are cousins. Walnuts, pecans, hickories all have a green fibrous husk surrounding the nut inside.

Speaking of hickories, hickory and pine nuts are edible, but I decided to include both of those trees in the utility tree chapter. The American chestnut and black walnut are also nut trees, but those were placed back in chapter one.

Oak

I decided to put oak in the nut chapter because everyone knows how important of a wood oak is, but people seem to forget that acorns are an incredibly important nut. In the first chapter I talked about the American chestnut. The mighty oak was the only tree capable of filling the void. Acorns feed all sorts of wild animals, and if you have pigs, acorn finished pork is considered a premium.

Here's the thing, you're able to eat acorns. It's been a long-standing historic source of food. Now in modern times we don't eat them, they're gross, but they are edible. The reason we don't like them is because the acorn nut is full of tannins. This makes it bitter, so to eat acorns, we have to wash those tannins out.

There are many different techniques to remove the tannins, and all of them are improved by grinding the acorns into a powder first. The best option is to rinse the tannins out and this can be done in one of two ways.

The first way is to put the acorns in a bowl of cold water. Leave it overnight. On the next day, drain the water and refill the bowl. Repeat this process for about a week, or until the water stays clear and the nuts taste "better."

The second method is to use running water. You can use your sink, but historically this was done by placing the nut powder in a bag and placing the bag in a stream or a creek.

Technique number two is simple, you boil the acorns. This can work, but the taste is still pretty rough if you do it this way.

The third method is to combine the nut powder with clay and ash. Yes, clay, as in dirt. The vitamins and minerals will absorb the tannins. You then cook the clay cakes and eat it, all of it, clay, ash, and acorn.

These methods are obviously only for survival reasons, but who knows, maybe you'll need to consume some acorns someday.

Oak wood, the most common hardwood in the world. Humanity uses oak for everything from firewood to furniture, but the tastiest use of oak is to use it for its smoking. Typically, when you smoke something, oak is the main source of smoke and then you add additional wood types to flavor that smoke.

Now let's go back to those tannins. The word tannin sounds similar to tanning, right? Well, have you ever heard of tanning leather? Tan, is the old Latin word for oak. Historically, how you would tan leather is by soaking oak bark in water and then using that water to tan the leather hide.

Latin: Quercus
Grow Zone: 3-10
Uses: Nuts, Tanning, Firewood
Growth Rate: 2ft
Season: Early Fall
Height: 40-80ft
Fruit: 20-50 years

PROs
Acorns
Firewood
Tannins
Smoking
Woodworking

CONs
Tannins

Hazelnut

Also known as filberts in some regions, hazelnuts are probably my favorite nut. Commercially most hazelnuts go to Nutella production, which I think is a shame because they are way better freshly cracked. But to be fair, that might be my personal bias. I hate chocolate.

The cool thing about hazelnuts is that the shells are actually a useful biofuel. Great for making biochar, or as a feedstock. The shells have a lot of btu's and are useful in pyrolysis. For those of you who don't know what pyrolysis is, overly simplified, it's using heat to acquire gasses and oils from materials. In our context, it's usually making charcoal for the garden. Speaking of the garden, hazelnut shells can be used as a mulch, but more importantly they're a snail deterrent.

Now the hazelnut tree itself is one of my favorites. The wood has a long history of being used for weaving baskets, building fences or as a wattle. This is because the tree is one of the best coppicing trees out there.

So, here's some quick definitions, a wattle is a wall made up of wooden branches weaved together. Wattle and daub homes are a type of mud hut. Coppicing is the act of cutting down a tree and letting it regrow from the stump. Hazelnut trees have a quick turnaround of 5-7 years, meaning you can harvest the wood every 5-7 years.

Another reason why I love the hazelnut tree is that it's the only commercial nut tree that can thrive in the shade. All the other nut trees that I know of, love the sun. Hazelnuts are small understory trees/shrubs. They've spent their whole existence in the shade. This means, I can plant a large tree next to one and then have two trees in close proximity.

Latin: Corylus
Grow Zone: 4-9
Uses: Nuts, Coppicing, Weaving
Growth Rate: 2ft
Season: Late Summer
Height: 15ft
Fruit: 3-4 years

PROs
Nuts
Firewood
Weaving
Shade

Almond

Ah, the humble almond. The world's favorite tree nut. 80% of the almonds in the world are grown in California, but the nut originates in the Mediterranean. Like I said at the beginning of the chapter, almonds are very closely related to apricots. Look at an apricot seed and compare it to an almond shell. They look similar. That said, almond, and apricot trees for that matter, are most commonly grafted onto a peach tree rootstock. This is done to improve production.

Quick definitions, grafting is the act of taking a branch from a tree you like, and attaching it to a young tree. The rootstock is that young tree, and it's usually a tree with good roots. Virtually every fruit tree you've ever seen has been grafted.

Now almonds, like most nuts, have an outer husk that protects the shell and nut while growing, luckily unlike juglone nuts, the nut falls out of the husk. This makes processing your nuts easier.

Oh, and screw your almond milk. Almond orchards don't provide enough nectar for bees. So, California has to import over 2 million boxes of bees, each season. Where they will work to the brink of starvation. Just enjoy the nuts and get a cow.

Latin: Prunus dulcis
Grow Zone: 5-9
Uses: Snacks
Growth Rate: 1ft
Season: Late Summer
Height: 10-15ft
Fruit: 3 Years

PROs
Tasty

CONs
Kills bees

Chestnut

I talked about the American chestnut tree previously, but now let's talk about chestnuts. Cause here's the thing, chestnuts arguably are the most important nut for the homestead. Early America was built off American chestnuts. China consumes a ton of chestnuts. Japan enjoys their chestnuts & so do Europeans. Anywhere that enjoys a temperate climate has a long history with chestnuts.

But why? Most nut trees produce in spurts. You get a ton of acorns one year and then the next several years, next to nothing. Walnuts, pecans, same thing. They do this so that the predatory population like squirrels and pigs stays low.

Speaking of pigs, this is why chestnuts are the most important nut. Sure, you and I can enjoy some roasted chestnuts on Christmas morning, but pigs...set your pigs loose in the nut grove and just watch them work.

There are four main types of chestnut, American, Chinese, Japanese, and European, but there's a fifth type, chinquapin. Chinquapins will get their own section and American chestnuts already got theirs. This section is for the three types that are commonly grown for nuts. European is the most cold-hardy, and Chinese is the most blight resistant. All are considered pretty tasty. All are great options to feed you and your livestock.

Latin: Castanea
Grow Zone: 4-8
Uses: Nuts
Growth Rate: 1-2ft
Season: Late Summer/Early Fall
Height: 40-60ft
Fruit: 3-5 years

PROs
Nuts
Blight resistant

Chinquapin Chestnut

The chinquapin. The dwarf chestnut. The cousin of the American chestnut. Not to be confused with the chinquapin oak, That's just an oak. The chinquapin chestnut gets its own section cause it's a little different from the rest. Chinquapins are mini chestnuts. The shrub is small, and the nuts are small.

Chinquapins are from the American South, specifically the Ozarks and are desired by wildlife and me. The nuts aren't grown commercially, because like the American chestnut, the blight is not their friend. They do handle it better than their cousin though, which is why they're still around. They also handle the shade. They even supposedly taste better than chestnuts. Unfortunately, they're a lot harder to gather and process with machines. Plus, growing them from seed can be tricky. More reasons why they're not grown commercially. But who cares? I don't have a big commercial nut harvester. I have my hands and a lot of shady spots on my property.

Latin: Castanea pumila
Grow Zone: 5-9
Uses: Nuts
Growth Rate: 1-2ft
Season: Late Summer
Height: 15-30ft
Fruit: 5-7 Years

PROs
Nuts

CONs
Small nuts
Blight vulnerable

Walnut

The English walnuts, also known as The Persian walnut, is what you picture when you think of walnuts. For a nut that can be bitter at times, it's one of the most popular nuts in the world. I enjoy it. I prefer its cousin the pecan more, but it's a good nut.

The walnut grows in a green husk, which has to be peeled off after harvest so that the nut can dry out. If you procrastinate this step, the flavor worsens.

Walnuts are part of the juglone family so be careful when planting them around other plants. When stressed the walnut tree will release juglone and try to kill the nearby competition. They're not as potent as black walnuts, but still keep juglone tolerance in mind.

Latin: Juglans regia
Grow Zone: 3-7
Uses: Snacks
Growth Rate: 2ft
Season: Early Fall
Height: 40-60ft
Fruit: 4-5 Years

PROs
Nuts

CONs
Juglone

Pecan

The humble pecan, surprisingly a way less popular nut compared to the walnut, even though flavor wise, it's one of my favorite nuts. This is because it is one of the most recent crops to be domesticated. Wild pecans are a common nut in the American South, but we only started cultivating them in the 1880's. My bet is that the northerners discovered how good pecan pie is.

Like the walnut, pecans grow in a green husk, and it must be peeled off so the nut can dry. And once again, pecans are part of the juglone family so be careful when planting them around other plants.

Latin: Carya illinoinensis
Grow Zone: 5-9
Uses: Snacks, Smoking, Pie
Growth 2-3ft
Season: Late Fall
Height: 70-100ft
Fruit: 4-8ft

PROs
Tastes good

CONs
Juglone

Butternut

The butternut is also a juglone tree, but this one is a little less known than the previous two. Also known as the white walnut, it's native to the northeastern part of the US. It gets its name because the most common way this nut was consumed is in a nut spread, like peanut butter. It's walnut butter. This is because the nuts are rich in oil. So, you press the nut for oil, and then enjoy the leftover buttery spread. Oh, and like many other hardwoods, the tree can be tapped for syrup.

Unfortunately, the butternut tree is endangered. The butternut canker is similar to the chestnut blight. A canker will grow and kill the tree. If left untreated, a wild butternut will die.

The husks were used as a dye. Black walnut husks were used for a dark color, butternut was used for a light yellowish color. Almost like butter...

Latin: Juglans cinerea
Grow Zone: 3-7
Uses: Winter Oil, Nut Butter, Syrup
Growth Rate: 1ft
Season: Mid Fall
Height: 4-60ft
Fruit: 2-3 Years

PROs
Less bitter than its cousins
Oil

CONs
Mild Juglone
Endangered

Heartnut

Japanese walnuts are awesome. The heartnut is a cultivated type of Japanese walnut. It got its name, because it grows in the shape of a heart, making it easier to split open. The best part about the heartnut is that unlike the English walnut, or the black walnut, it has no bitter aftertaste to it.

Latin: Juglans ailantifolia var. cordiformis
Grow Zone: 5-9
Uses: Nuts
Growth Rate: 3-4ft
Season: Mid Fall
Height: 50ft
Fruit: 3-6 Years

PROs
Fast Growing
Not Bitter

CONs
Juglone

Beech

The American beech tree, the least important nut tree on this list. Not to be confused with birch trees, which are completely unrelated. This is not a nut tree you will want to plant. It takes 50 years to start producing nuts, & the nuts are edible but not desired. However, if you already have a beech tree, it's a free source of nuts for your livestock or woodland creatures.

The beech tree is easy to identify. In the American eastern woodlands, there are only two trees that have a smooth bark. Holly is one, beech is the other. So, if it's a nut tree, with smooth bark, it's a beech. The special thing about beech is that it is incredibly shade tolerant. It will grow in shade conditions that other plants will struggle in.

Don't eat a ton of the nuts raw. You can have a few, but too many will give you issues. It's better to roast them.

Latin: Fagus sylvatica
Grow Zone: 3-9
Uses: Winter Fruit
Growth Rate: 1-2ft
Season: Fall
Height: 60-80ft
Fruit: 50 Years

PROs
Free Nuts

CONs
50 years

CHAPTER 4
WOOD TREES

This should be a shorter chapter. You see, most trees, even the best wood trees, have so many uses. Black locust and Mulberry are two trees included in chapter 1. They're also arguably the best trees to plant for firewood production. Most American homes are built out of pine, but pine is more than just a great source of lumber. I'll talk about that more in the utility chapter. However, that's not to say the trees contained in this chapter are only good for wood, just that I would say their primary use, their primary asset to the homestead, is for their wood.

Now all trees can be burnt, so by that definition, they all make great firewood. That said, obviously something like oak is better than something like cottonwood. IF, and I stress IF, you have access to both. The people out in the dry western states, relied heavily on cottonwood for firewood. Softwoods can burn just as good and just as clean as hardwoods.

So, any wood can burn, but here's a list of good firewood trees that are in other chapters

Black locust
Mulberry
Oak
Honey Locust
Eucalyptus
Ash
Fir
Spruce
Birch
Pine

Same goes for timber trees, you can build furniture and homes with a lot of different woods but here's the best from the other chapters.

Oak
Fir
Pine
Poplar
Paulownia
Black walnut
Maple
Chestnut
Black locust

Hickory

The hickory tree is synonymous with tough. If you want a handle, hickory has been America's go to for its entire existence. It's a straight grain and has excellent shock absorption. Perfect for wooden handles.

But we also love the taste of hickory. If oak is the main wood for smoking, hickory is the main smoke flavoring. Which is why I was excited to discover that my pine/oak forest was in fact, a pine, oak, hickory forest.

Now the hickory tree is closely related to the pecan, and like the pecan it is part of the juglone family. In fact, the hickory nut actually looks similar to a walnut. However, you will never find hickory nuts in the store. This is because the hickory nut is mostly shell, with very little meat, and is very difficult to get out.

Historically, how people would utilize the nut primarily was in one of two ways. The first method was to drink it. Instead of going through the painstakingly slow process of trying to separate the meat from the shell, people would just mash everything. You then dump it all into a pot, shells included, and boil it. This would make a lovely hickory broth. A hickory brew. You then drink the hickory brew to get the calories and nutrients from the drink, and then dump the sludge.

The second way hickory nuts are used is to press them for oil. This is specifically done with bitternut hickory, but it can be done with any type of hickory. The main reason bitternut is used, is as you might guess, those nuts are bitter and don't taste good in a brew. The second reason though, is because while most hickories are mostly shell and just a little meat, the bitternut is the opposite. So, there's a lot of fats that you can press out of the nut. Oh, and in case you're worried, the nut meat is bitter, not the oil. Hickory oil, and for that matter pecan oil, are popular culinary oils.

Latin: Carya
Grow Zone: 4-8
Uses: Wood, Nuts, Oil
Growth Rate: 1ft
Season: Late Fall
Height: 60-80ft
Timber Maturity: 40-50 Years

PROs
Tough wood
Smoking wood
Nuts
Oil

CONs
Juglone
Slow growing

Osage Orange

Growing up, there was an Osage orange tree next to the creek we liked to play in. We didn't know what Osage orange was, but we did know that those ball sized fruits made great toys.

The wood is fantastic. It's extremely hard, rot resistant, and burns very hot. It's one of the top BTU firewood's native to America. The only trees surpassing it being black locust, mulberry and live oak. It's twice as hard as oak and it even surpasses hickory. In fact, it is one of the hardest woods in the world.

As for its rot resistance, it is also considered one of the top rot resistant woods in the world. Its density, and its natural chemical resistance makes it durable against both moisture and insects.

The Osage loved making their bows out of its wood, hence the name, and the wood is also orange, hence the other part of the name. Another name for this tree is hedge apple. Before the invention of barbed wire. Farmers would create hedges of Osage orange to keep animals out or in. Planted as a hedge it grows thick, strong, tight, and has lots of thorns.

Latin: Maclura pomifera
Grow Zone: 4-9
Uses: Firewood, Outdoors, Fence post, Bows, Hedge
Growth Rate: 3ft
Height: 30-60ft
Timber Maturity: 5, 25 Years

PROs
Hedgerow
High BTU firewood
Rot resistance

CONs
Thorns

Red Cedar

So fun fact, the western red cedar, the eastern red cedar, & the European cedars, are all actually completely different plants. They're not even part of the same families, but they look and act so similar we call them all cedars.

If you live in America, everyone here knows that cedar is the wood you buy for outdoors. It's very rot resistant, and unlike black locust, which is the most rot resistant, cedar is actually easy to work with.

When you go to the store to buy cedar it's almost always western red cedar. That's because this cedar grows straight and the grains are also straight. This makes it easy to saw into lumber and boards. If you're over on the west coast, you might get some eastern cedar, even though that's actually a juniper. Odds are it will still be western, but if you do end up with eastern, effectively the only difference is you'll have a few more knots and swirls in your grain.

Cedar has been used for everything, from foundation posts to shingles on the roof. I helped build my grandparents' porch out of cedar boards. Basically, cedar is popular for anything wooden outside However, the best part about cedar is its smell. It has a strong scent that we humans love but insects hate. Oh, and fun fact, the inner bark of cedar trees was one of the most popular fibers for creating rope.

Latin: Thuja plicata, Juniperus virginiana, Cedrus
Grow Zone: 2-9
Uses: Outdoors
Growth Rate: 1ft
Height: 40-50ft
Timber Maturity: 100 Years

PROs
Rot resistance
Insect resistance

CONs
Slow growing

Live Oak

The iconic tree of the American South, and it's the most energy dense wood in the world! To put it into perspective, red oak is the most common firewood in the northern hemisphere and it has a BTU value of 26.4m. Cottonwood is pretty low. At its highest it is 17.1m. Live oak comes in at an insane 36.6. That means you need twice the amount of cottonwood chopped and stored to provide you the same amount of heat as you would live oak. Here's the catch, the farthest north you can even possibly push live oak is maybe zone 7. Zone 7 is where winter barely exists, it's winter for like 8 weeks max. Zones 8-10? Even less. So yes, live oak is an incredible firewood, but is only available in a location that barely needs it.

Why is it called live oak? Because it's an oak tree, it drops acorns. That said, unlike red or white oak trees, live oaks are evergreen. Evergreens don't shed their leaves in the winter.

Unfortunately, unlike other oak trees, the live oak grows all twisty and bendy. This makes for a pretty tree, but not a very useful piece of timber. Historically live oaks were used for the bottom of a ship, because that's the part of the boat where you actually wanted the wood to be bent.

Latin: Quercus virginiana
Grow Zone: 8-10
Uses: Firewood, Acorns
Growth Rate: 2ft
Height: 40-80ft
Timber Maturity: 15 Years

PROs
High BTU firewood

CONs
Only grows in hot climates

Ironwood

These trees are so tough that they're named after the metal that transformed the world. Now I'm not talking about desert ironwood, nor black ironwood; those are different trees, but similar. I am talking about a whole family of trees with the nickname ironwood, including hornbeam and hophornbeam.

These trees are tough, they were used for anything that needed to take a beating. The wood was used as gears in factories. Romans loved to make their chariot wheels with ironwood. In the American woodlands, the wood was even used as wooden nails. However, as a homesteader, you probably would only want this tree if you were using it to make wooden handles, and are wanting to plant it in an understory location or where planting the juglone producing hickory would be problematic.

Ironwood is a slow growing, understory tree. It is Incredibly shade tolerant. Hornbeam is also nicknamed the muscle tree, because it looks like it's made of smooth gray muscles. Hornbeam does not grow straight. Hophornbeam has flakey bark and grows relatively straight. Medicinally the bark was used for wounds. It helped stop the bleeding and had some pain killing properties. Oh, and they have small edible nuts.

Latin: Carpinus/Ostrya
Grow Zone: 3-9
Uses: Cogs, Handles
Growth Rate: 1ft
Height: 40ft
Timber Maturity: 30 Years

PROs
Tough
Nuts

CONs
Twisted

Black Cherry

Cherry wood doesn't come from your backyard cherry tree. Black cherry is a towering tree and not closely related to the cherry tree you know. The fruit of the Black cherry is edible, but unlike the choke cherry, it actually does taste like a cherry. It's just a tiny fruit, so typically it is used in jams and jellies.

Cherry wood is a popular wood for woodworking. Funny enough, out of all the popular cabinet and flooring woods used in America, cherry is the only one to make it into the wood tree chapter. Walnut, oak, and maple, all are great woods, but those trees have many different uses. Cherry is the hardwood tree you plant, with the full intention of cutting it down and turning it into furniture as soon as possible. It's also the fastest growing hardwood out of the bunch. Plus, cherry wood is considered one of the easiest hardwoods to work with and it's versatile.

As far as smoking meat, cherry is once again, a top choice. When you buy cherry wood for smoking, it's black cherry. However, even though black cherry and cherry fruit trees aren't super close cousins, they are close enough that if you don't want a black cherry, you can use fruit tree cherry wood for smoking and get the exact same effect.

Latin: Prunus serotina
Grow Zone: 3-9
Uses: Furniture, Smoking
Growth Rate: 2-4ft
Season: Early Fall
Height: 60-80ft
Timber Maturity: 40-50 Years

PROs

Fast growing
Furniture quality
Fruit

CONs

40 years to harvest

Cottonwood

Cottonwood trees were one of the most important homesteading trees out west. If you settled a piece of land, your long-term success depended on your cottonwood grove. The cottonwood tree is the number one source of firewood in the western half of the US. Now, just so those easterners don't yell at me, yes, cottonwood sucks compared to oak, maple or any of the other half a million hardwoods we have in the east. Cottonwood is a perfectly good wood, it burns clean, it doesn't pop, and unlike in the east, it's really the only good option out west.

The cottonwood tree grows very fast, is drought resistant, and is flood resistant. They grow along stream banks all across North America, including in the harsh southern desert. Do you see why it was critical to homesteads? It grows fast, endures the harsh conditions, and is a good source of wood for cooking and heating.

The cottonwood is part of the poplar family, and its leaves shake in the wind just like quaking aspens. It's really pleasant to watch. Also like the aspen, their leaves turn a golden yellow in the fall. Its name comes from its seeds. The tree produces cotton like strands to send its seeds sailing off in the wind. It's cool to see the fluff balls float around, but it makes a mess. Same with the branches. This is not a strong wood. The branches of this tree break all the time. So in a yard, this tree sucks. On a homestead, you can just go pick up firewood after a storm.

One last note, medicinally the cottonwood buds are used as a pain relief. They contain the same chemical compounds as willow bark, similar to aspirins.

Latin: Populus fremontii/deltoides
Grow Zone: 2-9
Uses: Firewood
Growth Rate: 5ft
Height: 100ft
Timber Maturity: 3-5 Years

PROs

Fast turnaround

CONs

Messy
Low BTU

Redwood

The towering sequoias. The fastest growing, rot resistant, timber trees in the world. Just imagine how the explorers felt when they reached them. These men were used to the dense eastern woodlands, but as they started walking, the trees disappeared and were replaced by the great planes. As they kept walking, they eventually reached the northern Rockies and a frozen, highland desert. The only trees around were lame short scrubby things, and a ton of sagebrush. But they kept walking and eventually reached the behemoths of the west. Redwoods and douglas firs towering 300 feet overhead. If they traveled south, they'd hit the giant sequoias, also huge. If I were them, I'd be shocked.

Redwoods are a wet loving tree that grows fast and straight. The are the perfect timber tree. Unfortunately, they are also the perfect timber tree. Back when California was booming, about 97% of the oldest and biggest redwoods were logged. San Francisco only exists thanks to redwoods. Another unfortunate thing about redwoods is that even though they are the perfect timber tree, they only grow in foggy wet environments. They don't like dry air. There's not a ton of land like that, so they can't be grown in most places. At least not on an industrial, plantation scale. As a homesteader, you might be able to baby this fast growing, water loving, timber tree.

The tallest living tree in the world is a redwood and it is a massive 380 feet tall. Just to put it into perspective, have you ever been in a skyscraper? A 30-story building, which is a big skyscraper, is only 300 feet. Those are built with reinforcements, steel, and concrete. Redwoods are made of... wood.

Latin: Sequoia sempervirens
Grow Zone: 7-9
Uses: Timber
Growth Rate: 2-6ft
Height: 300ft
Timber Maturity: 20 Years

PROs
Fast growing
Rot resistant

CONs
Likes fog

Tulip Tree

You will almost always hear this tree be referred to as a tulip poplar. The name is confusing though. It is not a poplar, even though its leaves flutter in the wind like poplars. It's actually a cousin to magnolia. It's also not a tulip, even though it produces these little yellow tulip-like flowers. So, it is also sometimes called the tulip tree or yellow poplar.

This is the most valuable, crappy, hard wood America has. What I mean by that is that tulip trees grow super-fast and straight. The wood is technically a hardwood due to its grains but it is actually only slightly harder than pine. It is "the" cheap hardwood. It's used for picture frames, pallets, and for plywood. Historically it is what you used for log cabins and dugout canoes. Speaking of canoes, the bark of tulip poplars could be used to make a bark canoe and for baskets. The bark is good for starting primitive fires too.

Latin: Liriodendron tulipifera
Grow Zone: 4-9
Uses: Cheap Hardwood
Growth Rate: 3-5ft
Height: 120ft
Timber Maturity: 20 Years

PROs
Easy to work with
Cheap
Strong

CONs
Soft

CHAPTER 5
UTILITY TREES

What makes a tree useful? Well, every tree in this book is useful for some reason or another. If it wasn't a useful enough of a tree then it got tossed on the discard pile. Some trees are useful for their fruit. Others are important for a specific task like nitrogen fixation or their wood. This chapter is for the more miscellaneous tasks like bubblegum or root beer.

Pine

One of the most common trees in the world and is arguably the most useful tree in the world. Pine is a homesteader's best friend and has been the friend of many survivalists & bushcrafters throughout the ages.

First, let's start off with the leaves. Pine needles are an incredible source of vitamin C. Just boil them up & enjoy the tea. There's also the pine straw. Pine straw is an incredible mulch. No pine needles do not make your soil more acidic; that's a myth & there are plenty of scientific papers disproving it. Pine needles are acidic yes, but by the time they break down into the soil, there is no acidity left.

Now unfortunately, pine needles don't break down easily. This is great for mulch, not so great for compost... or is it? Sure, in most cases, you want your compost pile to break down as quickly as possible, but sometimes you don't. For example, when you want heat.

Biomeiler is the act of heating structures, like a greenhouse, with compost. You see, compost gets very hot, and has been used as a passive source of heat for thousands of years. In modern times this technology was revolutionized by a French scientist named Jene Pane. He used compost like a boiler, to heat his home.

So, we've covered pine needles, but now let's move onto the bark, specifically, the cambium layer. This is the layer between the outer hard bark & the inner wood. This part of the pine bark is edible, and has been consumed as a survival food. In Scandinavian countries they even have a tradition of making pine bark bread. You don't have to make it into bread, you can eat it fresh. People all across the northern hemisphere would just cut strips off & eat it. You can even dry it like jerky. I've eaten pine bark before, and it tastes exactly how you would imagine. I hope you like the taste of pine needles, cause it's even stronger in the bark.

Speaking of food, there's also pine nuts. However, this honestly isn't a good source of calories. Pine nuts are tiny and difficult to extract from the pine cone. There's a reason why pine nuts are expensive and usually were harvested in a third world country where labor is cheap.

Now let's talk about what happens when the tree gets injured, specifically when the pine tree gets cut. You see when this happens, you gain access to pine sap–or pine resin–and pine resin is extremely useful. You can use it for everything from water proofing to glue. From fire starters to first aid & skin salves.

Obviously, the most important use of pine is its timber. Pine is used all across the globe for building structures and homes. It grows fast, straight, and strong. When the wood dries, it is less likely to warp and remains flexible. All attributes you want when building something out of wood.

Latin Pinus
Grow Zone: 2-9
Growth Rate: 2-3ft
Wood: Construction
Height: 100ft
Coppicing: No

PROs
Lightweight construction
Edible bark
Mulch
Vitamin-C
Pine resin

CONs
Messy

Aspen

Growing up, aspens were my favorite tree, and they still are one of my favorites, even if they didn't make it into my top 10 for this book. I just love the way they look. The way they shimmer in the summer. The way they turn yellow in the fall. I was born in Colorado and I grew up in Oklahoma. Oklahoma is predominantly pine/oak. Colorado is predominantly pine/aspen. Aspens always remind me of my birthplace. You should see Colorado in the fall. The mountains are covered in yellow leaves.

In the US, the most common type of aspen is the quaking aspen, but there's different types of aspens across the globe. The cool thing about aspen trees is that they are a natural sunscreen. One time I was up in the mountains of Idaho with my girlfriend and we were doing a road trip. The sun was beating down on my left arm. I could feel it burning and I did not bring any sunscreen. So, when we stopped to do some hiking, the first thing I did was rub my hands up and down on an aspen tree. I then rubbed that dust into my arm. It worked. I did not burn, and I definitely would have.

The other nice thing about aspens is that they provide very dappled shade, which basically means sunlight still gets through. This means plants underneath the aspen tree will still get sunlight. Aspens also happen to like a bit of shade, especially from that afternoon sun. Plant them to the north of another tree.

Now, this isn't important but it's pretty cool. Aspens like to make clones of themselves. An aspen tree will grow up, send roots out, and then at the edge of its roots, it'll start growing another tree. So quite often aspen forests are one tree that has grown multiple trunks from the same network of roots. In fact, the single biggest living organism in the world is an aspen and it's known as Pando. Pando is a forest of aspens that stretches across 106 acres and has 47,000 stems (trunks). It is one plant.

Latin: Populus tremuloides/tremula
Grow Zone: 2-8
Ornamental: Yes
Medicinal: Yes
Growth Rate: 2ft
Uses: Sunscreen
Height: 80ft

PROs
Pretty
Sunscreen

CONs
Tree gets sick easily

Sassafras

Sassafras! That's just a fun word to say. Sassafras is also arguably one of the most important trees ever to be discovered and no one is going to change my mind. Sassafras is the flavor responsible for root beer and sarsaparilla.

You see, the original root beers were made by boiling the roots of the sassafras tree. You then could add additional flavors like vanilla or licorice to the root beer. The most popular variant to root beer is sarsaparilla. Sarsaparilla's flavor is still mostly sassafras, but you would add in a chunk of sarsaparilla root to change things up.

Nowadays, root beer and sassafras flavors are artificially made through chemicals. This is because there was a study forever ago that said, if mice were fed an insane level of safrole, they would develop cancer. Safrole is the chemical found in sassafras. You're not a mouse and I doubt you drink that much root beer, but I digress.

The sassafras tree also is a cool looking tree, with a whole rainbow of colors in the fall. The leaves are uniquely shaped and, in the fall, they will turn any shade of red, yellow, or orange, on the same tree.

Latin: Sassafras albidum
Grow Zone: 4-9
Ornamental: Yes
Medicinal: Yes
Uses: Root Beer
Growth Rate: 3-4ft
Height: 30-60ft

PROs
Root Beer
Fall Colors

CONs
Cancer?

Yaupon Holly

Let's talk drugs. Not hard drugs. I mean caffeine, the most abused drug on the planet. The world's favorite sources of caffeine are tea and coffee. There's also yerba mate, which is popular in South America, and then there's always chocolate. Yaupon is the historical caffeine of choice for North America. It's native to the American southeast, from Texas to Florida, and was incredibly popular with the local tribes and the Spanish. It faded from popularity because of, um, let's say historical reasons. However, it is slowly making a comeback due to some advantages. First off, it grows well in the southern US. The only other option is the tea shrub. All other sources of the world's favorite drug grow exclusively in the tropics, and unlike tea leaves yaupon does not contain tannins, so you can't make your tea bitter by over boiling it. Which I guess is a thing. I've personally never had tea, just herbal teas, so I wouldn't know.

As you might guess by the name, yaupon holly is a relative of the holly tree. Holly itself isn't very useful, but the holly family is considered very pretty, especially when they have their red berries in the winter. You don't want to eat the berries but a lot of birds will thank you for them.

Latin: Ilex vomitoria
Grow Zone: 7-9
Ornamental: Yes
Medicinal: No
Growth Rate: 1ft
Uses: Caffeine
Height: 25ft

PROs
Caffeine

CONs
Addiction

Birch

This is the ultimate fire-starting tree. There are two main families of birch trees in the world, paper birch, and river birch. In America the paper birch is predominantly in the west, and up in the Rocky Mountains. The river birch is further back east, predominantly in the southern states, and, as you might guess, it likes growing along the river.

The bark of birch trees is very thin, and full of oils, making them excellent pieces of tinder. The paper birch bark is white and is as flexible as paper. This is the ultimate bushcraft bark for making containers and canoes.

The river birch bark is red, and loves to flake off, rolling up the tree. Due to this, I'd say the river birch looks more like a tree made of paper but I didn't get to name them. If you have a thicker chunk of bark, take your knife and scrape the back a few times. This'll make a highly flammable dust that can catch a spark.

The wood of the birch tree is great for fires as well. The wood is popular for making primitive fire tools like a bow drill. When using a bow drill, you need a lot of friction on a wood that isn't too tough, and preferably full of oil. As firewood, it dries and cures fast, and it burns at a medium warmth.

Now let's talk about chaga. Chaga is a mushroom that grows on birch trees. Keeping with the theme so far, chaga is the ultimate fire mushroom. It's a dense fibrous mushroom that loves to smolder. Bushcrafters will put a chunk of chaga in their flint kits. It can be used for friction fires, directly. If you're using a bow drill, drill right onto the chaga. If you're using a fire saw, saw back and forth, directly into the chaga. However, the most important use of chaga was for transporting and keeping embers.

Think about it, how much effort does it take to start a fire by rubbing sticks? The last thing you want to do is that, every single night, but if you had a chunk of chaga you could "light" it. Chaga will smolder for hours and was the best way to transport an ember with you. You could take it along with you as you walked and looked for a new campsite. You could also cook your food, ignite the chaga, and then go do other things, without worrying about keeping the fire alive. You knew that when it was time to cook again, the smoldering chaga would make it easy.

Medicinally, both the birch tree and the chaga mushroom have a lot of benefits. Like other members of the poplar family the birch tree has aspirin-like qualities, and can be used as a painkiller. The leaves are often used to help with sprains and inflamed skins. Chaga's main claim to fame is its incredibly powerful antioxidant capabilities. Which is sciencey talk for boosting your immune system and decreasing inflammation pain.

The last thing to mention is birch water. So, everyone knows you can tap maples for sap, but you can actually tap most deciduous trees. Birch sap typically isn't boiled down into a syrup, instead it is most commonly drunk straight, as a refreshing, slightly sweetened drink.

Latin: Betula papyrifera/nigra
Grow Zone: 4-9
Medicinal: Yes
Growth Rate: 2ft
Uses: Fire, Medicine
Height: 50ft

PROs
Bark
Fire
Birch water

Mastic

The mastic tree is a small, pretty, evergreen tree. Mastic gum was the original chewing gum of the ancient world. It has been used since Ancient Greece. As you might guess, this is a Mediterranean tree. It likes hot dry summers and is one of the few things still green during the summer. The berries are edible but not commonly consumed. It's been described as a tart raisin.

What people are really after is the resin. When you wound the mastic tree with a shallow cut, it produces mastic resin. Mastic resin has a lot of health benefits but the main reason people want it is for its chewiness. Again, it's the original gum. This gum is really good for you too. It helps your digestion, bad breath, and even oral health. The oil has antibacterial and antifungal traits so you can also use it to help with cuts and skin problems. Lastly, the leaves are a popular spice. People use them in everything from cheese to cakes.

Latin: Pistacia lentiscus
Grow Zone: 9-11
Ornamental: Yes
Medicinal: Yes
Growth Rate: 1ft
Uses: Chewing Gum
Height: 25ft

PROs
Chewing gum

CHAPTER 6
NITROGEN FIXERS

Let's define nitrogen fixer real quick. Plants need many different nutrients, but the three most important are NPK. N stands for nitrogen, and nitrogen is what is mainly responsible for the plants ability to grow, and to create proteins. Nitrogen is so important that certain species of plants are designed to take nitrogen from the air and put it into the soil. These plants have been dubbed nitrogen fixers. Usually, they are part of the legume family, think beans, and are high in protein, which is great for livestock. Although, due to this fact, they also tend to have thorns to defend themselves. Black locust being a prime example.

There's one key thing to remember about nitrogen fixation. When a nitrogen fixer takes nitrogen from the air and puts it into the soil, it is doing it for its own benefit. If you want that nitrogen to benefit your other nearby plants you have to coppice the nitrogen fixer to force it to share the nitrogen. Coppicing means to cut a tree, leave the stump, then you and wait for it to grow back, from the stump. Nitrogen fixers tend to grow back rapidly after being coppiced, or chopped down.

So, this is the chapter that will be full of invasive trees. Nitrogen fixers are typically aggressive resilient pioneer species. As far as nature is concerned, this is intentional. The job of a pioneer species is to attack damaged, nutrient depleted soils, and over the next few decades, rejuvenate that piece of land. Here's the problem, farmers hate aggressive, resilient pioneer plants. We call them weeds, and nitrogen fixing weeds are the most aggressive. Why? Because they have access to all that juicy nitrogen. It also doesn't help when they have those pesky thorns. People hate thorns, especially when those thorny weeds are growing somewhere we don't want them. Basically, please don't yell at me because I wrote about a useful tree that might be hated in your specific region. If it's not a good fit, pick a different one.

Honey Locust

The honey locust is the more popular sibling to the black locust. The black locust is my favorite, but for some reason, everyone else loves the honey locust. I don't blame them. The fall colors are beautiful, and the cultivated varieties of honey locust don't have thorns. In the wild, both have thorns, but a wild honey locust looks way too mean. Its nickname is the thorny locust. It has massive thorns, and its thorns have thorns. However, the domesticated varieties have a mutation that makes them thornless. So luckily for the honey locust, people like it now.

It's a popular ornamental tree, planted for its gorgeous yellow fall colors. It grows fast, and yes, it is a very good nitrogen fixer. It's not quite as good as the black locust, but it does a really good job. In fact, that is the story of the honey locust. It does what the black locust does, just less. It grows fast, but not quite as fast. It dumps a ton of nitrogen, but not quite as much. The same goes for its rot resistance, firewood capabilities, and flowers. However, it's also less of a pain. It's not as hard to keep in check. It doesn't have thorns, and the wood is easier to work with.

Now let's go back to those flowers. The black locust flowers are edible, the beans are not. The black locust flower nectar is considered a premium source for honey. Interestingly, the honey locust flowers… don't make good honey. They're tiny and not a good source of nectar for bees. Well then, why is it called the honey locust? I'm glad you asked. The bean pods on the honey locust are big and are a natural sweetener, like honey. I know. It's stupid. I didn't name the trees. That's just how it works.

The nice thing about the honey locust is that nothing on it is toxic. The black locust beans are, and if your animals eat too many of the black locust leaves, it can sometimes be problematic. Luckily, the honey locust has no such concerns. It's not as nutritious or desirable as the black locust, but it still is a fantastic source of feed, with none of the possible concerns of its cousin. My vote is, use both.

Latin: Gleditsia triacanthos
Grow Zone: 3-9
Ornamental: Yes
Growth Rate: 2-4ft
Animal feed: Yes
Wood: Rot Resistant
Height: 80ft
Coppicing: Yes
Nitrogen Fixer: Yes

PROs
Nitrogen
Seedpods
Wood

CONs
Wild Thorns

Alder

Alder is such an incredible nitrogen fixer. It's hard to measure the exact amounts of how much nitrogen a specific type of plant will deposit, but it's generally agreed upon that the black locust, honey locust, and alder, are the top dogs. The cool thing about alder is that it is a wetland loving tree. It's common to see it growing right on the banks of rivers and lakes. In fact, alder is very good at stabilizing banks and preventing erosion, but it's even cooler than that. You see, alder-cones, (think acorns) are actually beneficial for the water. They purify it, and lower the PH. We'll come back to that in a sec.

The wood of the alder tree is fairly rot resistant and is popular for woodworking. It also is popular for smoking. Salmon specifically is often cooked on top of an alder plank board. Historically alder was one of the most popular charcoals. Alder charcoal burns hot and clean, so it was used in metallurgy and gunpowder. Finally, alder logs make great mushroom logs. They excel at growing shiitake, oyster, and other wood loving mushrooms.

The other useful part of the tree is the flowers and nuts. When young, their flowers, known as catkins, were used to make a green colored dye. The internet loves to mention that this is what Robin Hood would have used to color his cloak. Once mature, its nuts are known as alder cones, and these are pretty cool. Specifically, the chemicals found in the cones are useful. They are a cleaning agent. They are great for wounds, great for cleaning countertops, great for fish tanks.

You can extract it by soaking alder cones in warm water. The water will turn a dark reddish brown. It has antibacterial and antifungal properties. So, you can use it to disinfect things, and it has the added bonus of lowering the PH for aquatic life. However, the most important use for alder tea is on your body. You see, not only does it disinfect, it also helps with aches and pains, but more importantly it toughens the skin. Historically, it was a common practice to soak your feet in alder tea at the end of winter, so that your feet would toughen up. That way you could walk barefoot in the woods during the summer. This was done all across the globe, and if you're like me, you probably enjoy walking around barefoot whenever possible. Oh, and soaking your feet would also help with athlete's foot.

Latin: Alnus
Grow Zone: 3-8
Growth Rate: 2-3ft
Wood: Rot Resistant
Height: 50ft
Coppicing: Yes
Nitrogen Fixer: Yes

PROs
Nitrogen
Wood
Water purifying
Wetlands
Smoking meat

Kentucky Coffee

The Kentucky coffee tree is NOT a nitrogen fixer! I included it in this chapter cause most people seem to think it is. This is due to the mis-belief that all legumes are nitrogen fixers. If you don't know what a legume is, think beans and peas. It's pretty much any plant with a pod. Most legumes are indeed nitrogen fixers, and some are better than others. Locusts are fantastic. Redbuds, and your garden beans, not so much. The Kentucky coffee tree, KC for short, is not even capable of nitrogen fixation. That said, it's still a pretty cool tree.

As you might have guessed, KC is used to make a coffee-like drink. It doesn't have any caffeine, and I guess is milder in flavor. The tree produces these massive bean pods, with nut sized beans inside. At the end of the year, when the pods are brown and the beans are hard, people would roast them and then grind them into a brown coffee-like powder. I've never seen the appeal of a drink like that, so now let's talk about the better use of these beans. When the beans are young and green they are a perennial food option. Like a lot of other beans, these are toxic when raw, but once cooked they apparently taste similar to fava beans. This is how the tree was predominantly used, but during the wintertime, people in Kentucky made drinks, hence the name.

Another nickname for this tree is the dead tree. That's because it stays dormant for half the year. It comes late in the spring, and goes early in the fall. This might make you not want to plant it, and I would agree. However, this does present us with a unique use. During the summer, you want shade to keep things cool. During the rest of the year, you want sunlight to warm things up. So, the KC has been used as a shade tree when people are trying to help regulate a micro climate. Oh, and during the summer the shade is dappled, meaning some light still gets through, which is good for the plant's underneath.

Latin: Gymnocladus dioicus
Grow Zone: 3-8
Growth Rate: 1-2ft
Animal feed: Yes
Height: 80ft
Nitrogen Fixer: No

PROs
Coffee Drink
Beans

CONs
No Nitrogen

Russian Olive

The hated Russian olive. If there's one tree that could be labeled as the most hated tree in the American west, it'd probably be the Russian olive. It's a thorny, gnarly tree, that refuses to die. Winter won't kill it. Severe drought won't kill it. It's just one stubborn tree. That is why people hate it. Which is unfortunate, cause it's such a beneficial tree.

So, the Russian olive is from eastern Asia and isn't actually an olive tree, its leaves just look the same. It has a long history of uses, but we brought it over to America to help prevent desertification and to stop soil erosion. It's doing its job, but now it gets hate for it. Like most nitrogen fixers, it grows in terrible soil and tries to improve it. We just have a lot of terrible farm soil and so it gets in the way.

The main uses of this tree historically were as a food source and as a medicinal plant. It produces these little red berries that you can eat. It was a common practice to eat the berries before a meal, because it helps with digestion. They were also dried and used to treat joint pain. In fact, the whole tree is a massive anti-inflammatory and digestive aid. So, it was commonly used to treat pain and discomfort.

Now, why do I like this tree? Because it is a cold desert tree that fixes nitrogen and produces food. Cold desert homesteads don't have a lot of options. Not many plants like having no water and extreme winters. Unfortunately, because cold desert places have limited options, the Russian olive is kicking butt and considered invasive in a lot of the states it is useful in.

Oh, and it doesn't mind the heat either, so in the USA it can be found all the way up north in Idaho and all the way down south to New Mexico.

Latin: Elaeagnus angustifolia
Grow Zone: 3-7
Ornamental: Yes
Growth Rate: 4-6ft
Height: 25ft
Medicinal: Yes
Nitrogen Fixer: Yes

PROs
Nitrogen
Medicinal

CONs
Thorns

Golden Chain

Also known as laburnum, the golden chain tree is a popular landscaping tree. That's because it produces these long chains of golden yellow flowers. Hmm, I wonder where it got its name from?

I almost put it in the ornamental chapter, cause while it is a nitrogen fixing tree, and it is used as a nitrogen fixer, the main appeal of this tree is for its pretty flowers. People love the flowers so much that they'll make arches out of the tree. The branches are very flexible, so what people do is coppice the tree, and then take the regrowth and weave them out. As the tree matures, you slowly get an arch filled with golden yellow flowers.

After the spring time the tree starts producing highly toxic seed pods. While the tree is still young, people will go out and clip them off, but once the tree gets too big, most give up. There are two advantages to doing this. First, the pods are toxic and you don't want that around livestock and children. The second, is because of how the tree works. You see, the flowers bloom early in the spring and then the tree goes through a rapid growth spurt. However, once summer hits, it spends all of its energy into growing the pods or the roots. If you clip off the pods, then it puts all its energy into the roots and in the spring time the tree will have a lot of extra energy to devote to a large flower display.

The nice thing about this nitrogen fixer is that it's a smaller tree so you can put it closer to structures if you want. That said, its mature size shouldn't matter. If you're using it for nitrogen fixation, then the tree needs to be coppiced on a regular basis. But, as an ornamental that you occasionally coppice for nitrogen, it's nice that it's not too big.

Speaking of letting it get big; the wood is highly prized. It has a nice yellow and brown color and is strong. Again, it's not a very big tree, so the most common use of this wood is in instruments or when it gets used in a lathe, to make small things like cups.

Now this nitrogen fixer can be grown in a wide array of climates and has the nice bonus of not having any real pests or diseases, but it definitely prefers a more stable, Mediterranean like climate. It doesn't like extreme cold, nor does it like extreme heat, it can handle it, but it doesn't like it. So, if you're up north, give it lots of sun. If you're down south, protect it from the afternoon sun.

Latin: Laburnum
Grow Zone: 5-7
Ornamental: Yes
Growth Rate: 2ft
Wood: Valuable
Height: 15-20ft
Coppicing: Yes
Nitrogen Fixer: Yes

PROs
Pretty
Nitrogen
Small

CONs
Toxic Seeds

Catalpa

Also known as the cigar tree and the fish bait tree, the catalpa is an okay nitrogen fixer. It definitely isn't a heavy hitter like alder, so don't expect the same results, but it does produce nitrogen and is a pretty cool tree for other reasons.

As you might guess by the name, fishermen love this tree. The catalpa is the host to the catalpa moth. Their caterpillars, also known as catalpa worms, are considered the ultimate fish bait in the American southeast. The tree will get utterly decimated by the worms. They eat every single leaf. That's okay, it's used to it. Once they're gone, it'll quickly regrow a new set of leaves.

The tree is native to the American Southeast but is popular all across the nation as an ornamental. Fortunately for some people, and unfortunate for others, the worms only are common in its native range. However, everywhere else it's still a pretty tree, and a nitrogen fixer. It gets lots of big beautiful white flowers and the pollinators love the tree.

Once the flowers mature, it forms super long thick bean pods, hence its other name, the cigar tree. The main historical use of the pods was to make a tea to treat bronchitis and coughing.

If you're going to utilize this tree the most common practice is to pollard it, which is a type of coppicing. When you coppice the tree, you get a nice nitrogen dump for your other plants, but it also helps the catalpa produce strong healthy leaves.

The wood is brittle and not very strong, so in stormy weather you might have some limbs snapping, but the heartwood of the tree is fairly rot resistant, so it's used for fence posts.

Latin: Catalpa
Grow Zone: 4-8
Ornamental: Yes
Growth Rate: 2ft
Animal feed: Fish
Wood: Fence posts
Height: 40-70ft
Coppicing: Yes
Nitrogen Fixer: Yes

PROs
Fish Feed
Pretty

CONs
Only has worms in its native range

Goumi

Now let's talk about fruiting nitrogen fixers. To be fair, goumi and the next two are more shrub than tree, but I included sea berry in chapter one, so I better include goumi here. Goumi berries are these little red berries that are a sweet-sour berry. Even if goumi wasn't an excellent nitrogen fixer, people would plant this shrub for its berries.

I've already talked about two of its cousins. The autumn olive in chapter two, and the Russian olive earlier in this chapter. All three berry bushes are good nitrogen fixers, but if you're worried about invasives, the other two are harder to control. Which is interesting, cause the goumi is nearly indestructible. It's highly drought tolerant, deer proof, doesn't care about soil quality and it loves to be pruned. Which is a good characteristic to have in a nitrogen fixer. However, my favorite characteristic is the fact that it is highly frost resistant. You see, a lot of fruit trees have a problem. If you get a late frost, it kills all the flowers and you won't get any fruit that year. Goumi rarely struggles with this, and goumi berries are ripe early in the year. It's usually around the same time as strawberries. Its cousin the autumn olive, matures in the fall. Too bad they didn't name the Goumi, "spring olive." That would have made sense to me.

Latin: Elaeagnus multiflora.
Grow Zone: 4-9
Growth Rate: 2-3ft
Height: 10-15ft
Coppicing: Yes
Nitrogen Fixer: Yes
Fruit: 3 Years

PROs
Fruit
Nitrogen

Bayberry/Wax Myrtle

Let there be light. Wax myrtles, also known as northern or Southern bayberries, are a fruit producing shrub. The name "wax myrtle" is used in the southern states, and "bayberry" is used up north. They're describing the same plants. That said, these are not berries you want to eat. Wax myrtle is used for wax, hence the name. You boil the berries to extract the wax and then you make candles out of it. It is a nitrogen fixer and it is used as a pretty evergreen hedge. Medicinally, a tea was used to treat skin irritation.

Latin: Myrica pensylvanica/cerifera
Grow Zone: 3-8/7-9
Ornamental: Yes
Medicinal: Yes
Growth Rate: 3-5ft
Height: 20ft
Coppicing: Yes
Nitrogen Fixer: Yes

PROs
Candles
Nitrogen
Evergreen

Buffalo Berry

The buffaloberry, also known as the soapberry. Both names are good descriptors of this shrub. Now there's two main types of buffaloberry berries. Canadian and silver. Silver has thorns, Canadian does not, but silver buffaloberry is probably the one you want.

Soapberry. This name is due to high levels of saponins. In case you're a normal person, and have no idea what that means, saponins act kinda like soap. They lather, they bind onto grease and dirt, and they taste kinda... soapy. Both varieties have high levels of saponins but the Canadian soapberry is so high, you typically don't want to eat it. It's a utility tree, not a snack. The silver buffaloberry still has plenty of saponins, but way lower, and so it is often eaten. If you are going to eat it though, wait till after the first frost. It doesn't taste very good before then. That's the cool thing about this shrub. It's a winter fruit.

Now let's talk about the name, buffaloberry. Remember those saponins? They're antioxidants, and antioxidants are effectively a preservative. Antioxidants preserve you, and more importantly, they helped preserve pemmican. Pemmican was the fuel of the frontier. Pemmican is dried meat, ground up into a powder, combined with rendered fat. By itself that's a pretty shelf stable food. Buffaloberry was mixed with the dried buffalo meat and fat, and those saponins helped preserve the pemican even longer.

Now for the downsides. Silver buffaloberry is the one you want to use for food, but it has a ton of thorns, bears absolutely love them, and finally, only the females produce fruit, but a male is required to pollinate.

Latin: Shepherdia
Grow Zone: 3-8/2-6
Ornamental: Yes
Growth Rate: Fast
Animal feed: Yes
Height: 10ft/20ft
Coppicing: Yes
Nitrogen Fixer: Yes

PROs
Fruit
Pemmican
Soap

CONs
Gross

CHAPTER 7
MEDICINAL TREES

So here's the thing about herbal remedies: am I a doctor? No. Do I personally think they work? Absolutely. Legally you can't make any claims about medical benefits without a ton of studies and big pharma ain't gonna fund a study on a plant that you can grow in your backyard. So this chapter is purely for entertainment value, and I have no proof any of it works... even though people have been using these plants for medicinal purposes for thousands of years.

Personally, a doctor has never been able to help me with any chronic health issues, neither mentally nor physically. However, nutrition, medicinal plants, and healthy habits have. Now don't get me wrong, doctors have their place, especially when it comes to emergencies, surgeries, or when you have to go to the evil dentist's office. But with herbal remedies I've been able to eliminate any and all health problems I have dealt with for most of my life. My favorite medicinal "plant" is a mushroom called lion's mane. It did wonders for my brain, and is pretty tasty. That being said, if you decide to try a medicinal plant just because some dude wrote a paragraph on it in a book, without doing more research, consulting professionals, and/or understanding how it works... you're kinda dumb. Do more research.

Ginkgo

The ginkgo tree is really cool. It's medicinal, ornamental, and an edible nut tree. In the fall, the leaves turn a brilliant yellow and its stinky nuts are ready for harvest. When I say stink, I mean, don't plant a female Ginkgo tree anywhere near where you might be. Ginkgo nuts are a popular nut to eat, but the rotting husks are described as smelling like dog poop and vomit. However, don't let that discourage you; ginkgo is an awesome tree. Male trees don't produce the stink, but people will purposely plant females for the nuts.

Now nuts aren't the only reason this is a useful tree. You might've guessed that its main use is medicinal and the medicinal part of the tree is its leaves. The herb is known as ginkgo biloba and it's a super powerful brain booster. It can improve memory, is mood stabilizing, lowers anxiety, promotes better cognitive function, and can reduce mental decline associated with age. It has been known to help with PMS symptoms, and can improve circulation too.

Latin: Ginkgo biloba
Grow Zone: 3-9
Ornamental: Yes
Medicinal part: Leaves
Growth Rate: 1-2ft
Height: 50-80

PROs
Brain boost
Fall colors
Nuts

CONs
Stinky nut husks

Elderberry

The ultimate cold medicine. It has many other apparent benefits, but the main reason why elderberries are planted is because it is the cold medicine tree. Sore throat? Stuffy nose? Allergies? Elderberry. Now, it's more than just an anti-congestant. In addition to relieving symptoms, it's also a good immune booster. Basically, what this means is that elderberries can help you once you're sick, but it also can help prevent it.

Now, don't take too much, it's a laxative. So, if you're constipated, lots of elderberries. Otherwise, just a little elderberry. Also, don't eat it fresh off the bush. Elderberries should be turned into jam or syrup. When raw, they are mildly toxic, and generally people will feel nauseous after eating them.

Speaking of eating them, it's not just medicine. Lots of people enjoy eating elderberry jam as a snack. Like most berries, it has plenty of health benefits like being anti-inflammatory and an antioxidant.

Latin: Sambucus
Grow Zone: 3-9
Ornamental: Yes
Medicinal part: Berries
Growth Rate: 2-3ft
Height: 12-16ft

PROs
Cold medicine

CONs
Semi-toxic when raw
Laxative

Elm

The most potent elm is slippery elm, but as far as I'm aware, all elms work to some degree. Slippery elm gets its name because when you chew on the inner bark, it'll coat your throat with a nice soothing substance. This is great for sore throats.

Elms aren't just medicinal, they're also food! Elm bark in general is edible, and can be used as a survival food. The leaves are edible. The younger the better. The seeds and seed pods are too. Specifically, the Siberian elm seed pods are commonly consumed as food in China. You can also use elm bark to make rope.

Latin: Ulmus
Grow Zone: 3-9
Ornamental: Yes
Medicinal part: Bark
Growth Rate: 2-3ft
Height: 60ft

PROs
Sore throat
Food
Rope

Toothache Tree

So, there are several trees nicknamed the "toothache tree," but there's really only one toothache tree and then a lot of cousins. Hercules club, known as the toothache tree, will numb your mouth when consumed. Not just a little numbing; substantial, pain vanishing, numbing. You can chew on the leaves or the inner bark of the branches, both actions will numb your mouth. Dried bark will still work great too. This will not fix your dental problems. All it does is numb your mouth so you can't feel anything, that's it.

Note, it will not work as a numbing poultice. If my wrists hurt and I put some on, nothing will happen. It only works in soft open tissue like your mouth. The numbing effect only lasts for about 30 minutes. That's enough time for an old frontiersman to take some pliers to his tooth. In your case, you can use it to take the edge off while you wait for your appointment. Now, let's be clear. Go. Get. Your. Tooth. Fixed. If you're in enough pain that you need to numb it, you should go get an appointment.

Unfortunately, this bad boy is only able to grow in a hot humid subtropical kind of area. Luckily, the rest of you aren't quite out of luck. Hercules club is a Zanthoxylum. Remember how slippery elm is the most medicinal elm? Hercules club is the most medicinal Zanthoxylum, but it also has cousins.

For example, the devil's walking stick grows further up north, and the berries will give you a small numbing effect. In fact, have you ever heard of Sichuan peppers? Zanthoxylum berries are Sichuan peppers. In China, the dried berries are combined with really hot dishes so that the mild numbing effect will play havoc on your taste buds. In China they use two different Zanthoxylums for their spices. In America we have Hercules club down south and the devil's walking stick up north. There's also Zanthoxylum fagara, better known as wild lime or prickly lime-ash. Chewing on the leaves won't numb your pain, but it is supposedly incredible at eliminating bad breath.

Latin: Zanthoxylum clava-herculis
Grow Zone: 7-9ft
Ornamental: No
Medicinal part: Leaves & Branches
Growth Rate: 2ft
Height: 50ft

PROs
Numbs pain
Spice

CONs
Small range

Clove

On the subject of dental health, clove is the second most famous plant, besides mint. Clove will slightly numb your pain but it's nothing in comparison to the previous tree. However, clove does more than just numb things. It's anti-bacterial, anti-microbial, anti-inflammatory, blah blah blah blah. Basically, clove is fantastic for oral health. I use a mouthwash that contains a decent amount of clove oil. I've personally used clove for cold sores. It stings, but man does it work. Clove is good for earaches, and nausea.

Of course, clove is also a popular culinary herb. It has a nice sweet spicy flavor, very popular in Indian, Thai, or holiday cuisines. Speaking of India, that's where most of the clove trees are grown. It's more of a tropical tree and requires being harvested by hand. The clove bud is the flower bud, and it has to be harvested just before it blooms. If you're not in the tropics you can grow clove in a pot.

Latin: Syzygium aromaticum
Grow Zone: 11-12
Flowers: 6-10 Years
Medicinal part: Flower Buds
Growth Rate: Slow
Height: 25-40ft

PROs
Tasty
Oral health

CONs
Takes a while to produce

Linden

The relaxing tree. Stress, hysteria, insomnia, depression, hypertension, this is what linden is for. Also known as basswood, linden is good for mental health. It soothes things. It soothes your adrenal system. It soothes your muscles. People would rub linden teas on sore or tight muscles. It apparently even helps with blood pressure, but I would guess that's due to reduced stress. Linden's job is to get you to relax.

It's also a very popular ornamental tree, so you can find it in most cities. It's not anything spectacular looking, but it's a good basic tree. The seeds can be used to make a chocolate, coffee, mocha-like flavored drink and the inner bark was historically popular for making rope. It likes to grow in rocky, mountainous soils along river banks. That's useful, because not all trees like that terrain.

Latin: Tilia
Grow Zone: 3-9
Ornamental: Yes
Medicinal part: Flowers & Leaves
Growth Rate: 1-2ft
Height: 50-80ft

PROs
Pretty
Relaxing
Insomnia
Blood pressure
Rope

Frankincense

Now the actual name of the tree is boswellia, but since none of you have heard of the word boswellia, I called this section frankincense. Boswellia is the tree. Frankincense is the crystalized resin that comes from the tree.

Throughout history, frankincense was more expensive than gold. Why? Inflammation. Pain. You see, willow is a pain number, but anti-inflammatories remove the source of pain. There's lots of anti-inflammatory plants but frankincense is definitely considered one of the top dogs. Frankincense helps you heal faster too. Skin problems? Scars? Frankincense helps. Joint pain? Frankincense. Sore? You get the point. People use it for arthritis and as a blood thinner.

Now let's talk about the brain. The main use of frankincense historically was to burn it or to smell it. Frankincense helps your brain a lot, and it also helps out your endocrine system. That's a fancy word for hormones. Hormones control a lot. Emotions, focus, memory, these all get a boost.

The main reason frankincense is burned in churches or other holy places is because it helps you focus, it helps with meditation, and it soothes your spirit. It also smells good, which was even more important back when everyone was outside, sweating all day. Personally, I think that was one of the main reasons it was so valuable.

Back to boswellia. They are tough trees. You kind of have to be when your natural range is Africa & Arabia. It's said boswellia's will grow out of a rock if they have to. They don't need a lot of water and are very adaptive. Oh, & they love the heat. Unfortunately, they're hard to get started. Their seeds don't like to germinate for some reason. So, boswellia trees are kind of expensive.

If you decide to try growing one, you can grow it in a pot, but they definitely prefer being in the ground. Also, make sure it's one of the five types of boswellia trees that are grown for frankincense.

Latin: Boswellia
Grow Zone: 10-13
Ornamental: No
Medicinal part: Resin
Harvest rate: 8-10 Years
Height: 26ft

PROs
Smell
Pain
Easy to maintain

CONs
Hard to start

Myrrh

You knew this was coming. Once again, the tree is called commiphora, but you've never heard of that. Myrrh has a lot of similarities to frankincense, but also a few key differences. They're both incense, meaning they smell good. They both are pain killers. They both come from the crystallized resin of their trees. Both have religious significance. As an incense, myrrh has a more grounding effect than frankincense, but both are good at getting you in a reflective prayerful mood. Lastly, both come from the same region.

During the time of Jesus Christ, myrrh was considered one of the most powerful healing medicines in the region. The rich would put myrrh on wounds to help them heal. It's a pain killer and it also kills all the bad stuff, like bacteria, fungal, microbial, even boils. Outside of just wound care, myrrh had three main uses. The first two are foot and oral health. Use myrrh to treat any fungal issue, including athletes' feet. Candida is that white filmy stuff on your tongue. Candida makes your breath stink and is bad for your oral health. Candida is a fungus and myrrh does a very good job at treating it. It also helps with gum disease, and for the longest time, myrrh was used as a toothpaste. Myrrh aids with digestion. Finally, it can also help with period pain.

The third use of myrrh historically was for burials. Corpses stink. Myrrh was so good at fighting off all the decomposers and the scent of incense kept the body smelling good for long enough that you could have a funeral. Not really something we need these days, but it is kind of interesting.

Commiphora trees are incredibly thorny things; and they love the desert. So, as you might have guessed, they are very tough trees. The nice thing about commiphora is that they grow in pots. Lots of people will grow commiphora as a bonsai tree. I like this because it means, even if you're not a hot desert person, you can still consider growing it.

Latin: Commiphora
Grow Zone: 10-13
Ornamental: No
Medicinal part: Resin
Growth Rate: Medium
Height: 12ft

PROs
Healing
Anti-fungus
Oral health
Smells good

CONs
Thorns

Tea Tree

Tea tree/melaleuca is one of my favorite herbs. I use tea tree oil and rosemary on a constant basis. Now, just in case you didn't know, tea tree and the tea you drink are not remotely related. Tea tree is a medicinal plant in the myrtle family, and is from Australia. The tea bush is from India and is the caffeine plant everyone loves to drink. Don't drink tea tree. It does wonders on the outside, not so much on the inside.

In Australia It's also known as the paper bark tree and can be found growing along rivers or in the swamp. It loves wet soil. It looks like a conifer, think pine needles, but it isn't. A conifer has cones, like pine cones. Melaleuca has quite the impressive display of white flowers. When it's in bloom, the Australian river banks are apparently very pretty.

Historically, people would use the needles to help with breathing ailments. You can crush up the leaves and breathe in the fumes. This will clear up a stuffy nose, or help with congestion. However, the more effective method was to steam them, and then breathe in the steam.

The needles can also be used as a wound cleaner. People would make teas and wash their wounds or even just make a powder to rub into them like a paste. Tea tree is a good killer of the bad stuff.

In modern times, people use tea tree oil to make cleaner sprays for their bathrooms and kitchens.

Now let's talk about why I love this plant. My scalp loves it. My skin loves it. Tea Tree is very good at maintaining healthy hair, scalp, and skin. Teenagers love it because it helps with acne. I love it because it keeps my head from being itchy and it eliminates my dandruff problem.

Latin: Melaleuca alternifolia
Grow Zone: 7-9
Ornamental: Yes
Medicinal part: Leaves
Growth Rate: 2ft
Height: 25ft

PROs
Scalp health
Breathing
Wound cleanser
Cleaner

Witch Hazel

Speaking of dandruff and acne, now let's talk witch hazel. This is predominantly a North American tree, but there are some varieties from other places too. Witch hazel is used as a skin ointment. You can use it to treat rosacea or acne. It'll soothe shaving burns or any inflamed skin. You can use it as a moisturizer. You can use it to soothe an itchy scalp and to treat dandruff. You can even use it to reduce the itchiness of bug bites. This is predominantly due to it being an astringent. In the cosmetology world, astringent means it shrinks your skin's pores and removes excess gunk, aka, it cleans your face.

Besides the fact that it blooms in the fall, witch hazel has nothing to do with spooky season. It gets its name from the old English word "wiche," and that just means bendy. It's a bendy tree. That said, the flowers are totally witchy! Look them up, they're pretty interesting looking. The flowers bloom in the late fall. So, after most of the leaves have turned brown and fallen to the ground, there is still some color left in the forest and it's the witch hazel flowers. Oh, and speaking of the flowers blooming so late in the year, this is one of the last sources of nectar that bees get before winter. Also, the flowers in combination with the yellow leaves make witch hazel a popular fall ornamental.

Last fun little fact. Water witchers used witch hazel as a dowsing rod to try and find water. I'm not going to delve into that subject, but again, that's somehow not where it got its name.

Latin: Hamamelis
Grow Zone: 3-9
Ornamental: Yes
Medicinal part: Leaves & Bark
Growth Rate: 1-2
Height: 20-30

PROs
Dandruff
Skin
Bee food

CONs
Not spooky

Balm of Gilead

Just so we are clear. The balm of Gilead is a very specific ointment from a very specific place and from a very specific time. Some people want to call cottonwood buds the balm of Gilead, but that is simply not remotely accurate. Do some other plants have pain revealing properties? Yes. That doesn't make them the historical ointment.

Unfortunately, we don't know exactly what the balm was. Some scholars think it was the Arabian balsam tree, which is a type of myrrh. Other scholars think it was the terebinth, which is a cousin of the mastic tree. All these trees have incredible healing properties, but we don't know exactly what the balm was. That said, do you want to know what my uneducated wild guess is? I would assume it was a healing blend of multiple healing trees and herbs... kind of like what people do today. Anyway, I just wanted to mention these two trees so that maybe you could concoct a balm similar to the renowned balm of Gilead.

Balsam
Latin: Commiphora gileadensis
Grow Zone: 10-12
Ornamental: No
Medicinal part: Resin, Leaves, Bark
Growth rate: Slow
Height: 12ft

Terebinth
Latin: Pistacia terebinthus
Grow Zone: 10-12
Ornamental: Yes
Medicinal part: Resin, Leaves, Bark
Growth rate: Slow
Height: 16ft

PROs
Healing

CONs
Slow growing

Cypress

There are many different types of cypress. Bald cypress is loved in southern swampy areas. Leyland cypress is considered one of the fastest growing windscreen or privacy trees out there. The Mediterranean cypress and the blue cypress are the two most commonly used for making cypress oil. Cypress relieves pain, including menstrual. It promotes circulation, strengthens arterial walls, and helps relieve congestion. If you have a cold, cough, or stuffy nose, make some cypress tea. The wood is decently rot resistant so you can use it for some outdoor projects.

Latin: Cupressus
Grow Zone: 5-10
Ornamental: Yes
Medicinal part: Needles
Growth Rate: 2-4ft
Height: 80ft

PROs
Circulation
Relieves congestion
Pain relief
Hedge
Decorative
Rot resistant

Arborvitae

Also known as thuja, arborvitae is similar to cypress and is used as an evergreen privacy hedge. It looks similar to a cedar or a juniper tree, and the leaves are used to make a tea. If you have congestion in your throat the tea is good at removing phlegm. Like cypress it also helps with menstrual cramps. It's good for the hair, and helps with arthritis, but my favorite thing about this tree is that you can use it as an insect repellent. You can also use it as a cleaner. The wood was historically used for canoes, but nowadays people mostly use it for posts or poles. The oil that comes from arborvitae isn't just medicinal, it also is a decent water proofer for other woods. (don't use expensive "essential oil" for waterproofing.)

Latin: Thuja
Grow Zone: 2-7
Ornamental: Yes
Medicinal par: Needles
Growth Rate: 3-4ft
Height: 50-60ft

PROs
Relieves congestion
Pain
Hair
Hedge
Insect Repellant
Water proofing
Cleaner
Rot resistant

Spicebush

Spicebush has pretty yellow flowers in the spring, similar to forsythia. In the fall, it has brilliant yellow colors. It likes moist soil and grows in anything from full sun to pretty decent shade. The red berries are spicy... who would have guessed? Its flavor is described as peppery, similar to a lemon pepper rub, or as a replacement for allspice. The bark is used as a mild substitute for cinnamon. Spicebush smoke is even supposed to be tasty.

Now, the main medicinal use of spicebush was for its ability to break fevers, but people would also use the berries to make a salve for arthritis. You can also make spicebush tea. Supposedly it tastes pretty good, kills parasites, and helps with dysentery.

Latin: Lindera benzoin
Grow Zone: 4-9
Ornamental: Yes
Medicinal part: Leaves, Berries, Bark
Growth Rate: 1-2ft
Animal feed: Yes
Height: 15ft

PROs
Pretty
Tasty
Fever
Parasites
Pain

Hawthorn

Hawthorn is a small berry tree. Hawthorn trees are popular ornamental trees, and come in tons of different varieties, with different colored flowers and shapes. In the fall, hawthorns have bright fall colors and bright red berries. Most people think the berries are the medicinal part, and they are, but the flowers and leaves are just as effective. Hawthorn is good for the heart, particularly for heart pains and for blood pressure. You can consume the berries for medicinal purposes, but you can also just consume them as a berry. People use them to make jams.

Hawthorn is very thorny and so it was used as a hedge for a long time. The biggest downside of this tree though, is that it can stink in the spring. Depending on the variety, hawthorn flowers are said to smell like the plague.

Latin: Crataegus
Grow Zone: 4-8
Ornamental: Yes
Medicinal part: Flowers, Berries, Leaves
Growth Rate: 1-2ft
Height: 30ft

PROs
Blood Pressure
Heart
Jam
Pretty
Hedge

CONs
Stink
Thorns

CHAPTER 8
HOT CLIMATE FRUIT

The original name for this chapter was "tropical fruits," and that is an accurate name. The tropical belt is a geographical area that stretches across the whole globe. There are deserts, rainforests, and savannahs, all within the tropics. That said, when you say the word tropical, everyone immediately pictures a dense humid jungle. The trees in this chapter include everything from Mediterranean fruits, to the tropical rainforests in the far east.

Citrus

Citrus is the most desired family of fruits in the world. There are a few dozen types of fruits grown, everything from oranges to lemons. Now technically, the majority of citrus fruits were bred into existence by man. The pomelo, the citron, and the mandarin are the original grandparents of most citrus varieties.

Citron is sour, so the sour citrus fruits have a lot of citron in them. Pomelo is the sweet one. Grapefruit and oranges are mostly pomelo. The original mandarin didn't taste good but it was easy to peel. What we call mandarins today are a cross between pomelos and the original mandarins. Tangerines and clementines are in the mandarin branch.

Pomelo tastes delicious, but peeling it is an utter nightmare. So, we bred it with mandarins to make it easier. Grapefruit, sour orange, blood orange, and navel oranges are all part of this branch.

Citrons have that lovely sour factor, but we bred them with the children of mandarins and pomelos to get things like lemons and limes.

I barely scratched the surface here. There are dozens of types of citruses. Just in the lime family alone, there's key lime, finger lime, and of course lime. They all taste different. Off by itself, the kumquat is a weird citrus. The skin is the sweet part and the flesh is the sour part. Trifoliate orange is the most cold hardy of the citrus, and is typically used as a rootstalk when you're trying to grow citrus in the subtropics. However, it has fruits that are similar to lemon.

Latin: Rutaceae
Grow Zone: 8-11
Growth Rate: 1-2ft
Season: December
Height: 20ft
Fruit: 3-5 Years

PROs
Can be grown in a pot

Loquat

Loquat is not a citrus. It's a stone fruit, like apricots and plums. The name is similar to kumquat, but this fruit is more like a mild pear flavored peach. They come in both sweet or sour versions. Its sourness or sweetness depends on when you harvest it. The legend behind the loquat is that the trees line the river banks in China. When the fruit falls, it flows down the river and is eaten by carp. Those carp would gain great strength from the loquat and swim up the river to become dragons.

Latin: Eriobotrya japonica
Grow Zone: 8-11
Growth Rate: 1ft
Season: February
Height: 30ft
Fruit: 1-2 Years

PROs
Easy fruit

Fig

The most ancient of fruits. One of mankind's original crops. Adam and Eve even made aprons out of fig leaves. Fun fact about that, fig leaves are incredibly itchy and that's something a tormentor would encourage wearing.

If you thought apples had a wide range of variety, you'd really be impressed by the diversity of figs. That said you can mostly group them into two categories. Light and dark. This has nothing to do with the outer skin color, but the flesh. Light figs, or sugar figs, are super sweet. Dark figs have that berry flavor.

The tree is one of the most drought tolerant fruits humanity has, and if you're in a colder region, it can be grown in pots. If you're in a hot climate, the fig tree will actually produce two separate crops a year. Food can be wrapped in the leaves when cooking. This will give the food a slight coconut flavor. Finally, no there's not a dead wasp in your fig. Yes, the fig wasp dies in figs. The fig wasp is only in the Mediterranean and it's digested by the fig anyway.

Latin: Ficus carica
Grow Zone: 7-11
Growth Rate: 3-4ft
Season: Summer, Fall
Height: 30ft
Fruit: 3-5 Years

PROs
Variety
Two crops

CONs
Dislikes humidity

Banana

So a banana tree isn't actually a tree. They can grow 40 feet tall, but technically they are an herb and don't have any wood. Their trunk is just old shoots wound tightly together. Banana trees need a lot of fertilizer. They grow super-fast, and that growth needs fuel. In fact, because banana trees grow so fast, you can grow them from stumps in subtropical environments, but you'll have to protect the stumps each winter.

Have you ever had banana flavored candy and noticed it tastes nothing like banana? That's because that flavor is the old banana variety. You see, supply chains crave consistency, and so every banana is a clone. They are all Cavendish bananas.

By the way, cloning fruit isn't weird. We've been doing it for thousands of years. Every honey crisp apple tree is a clone of the original honey crisp apple tree. You clone a plant by taking a cutting and grafting it onto a root. This works great until a blight attacks a plant, and all the clones are identical, so they all die.

This is what happened to the banana. Before 1950 the banana everyone ate was the Gros Michel, but then a fungus known as the Panama disease wiped most of them out. You can still grow Gros Michels, they're just not in mass production anymore. You can grow Cavendish if you want, but there's tons of other banana varieties out there for you to try.

Latin: Musa
Grow Zone: 10-12
Growth Rate: Lightning Fast
Season: Year-round
Height: 20ft
Fruit: 15-18 Months

PROs
Fast
Year-round
Ornamental

CONs
Requires a lot of fertilizer

Tamarind

Tamarind is such an interesting fruit. Apparently, there's sweet versions, but all I've ever had are the sour ones. This is a natural sour patch kid. It's a sweet and sour fruit that tastes like candy. It looks... like a turd, but it tastes pretty good. It's a bean pod with a thin outer skin, that you peel off. You then peel off these weird vein things and you're left with this brown inner flesh and some big rock like seeds. You can eat it as a treat or you can use it in drinks.

Tamarind trees can grow to be massive things. They're nitrogen fixers. They originate in Africa and can handle very dry conditions, but nowadays they're spread all across the tropics, including wet humid regions. It's almost like people like candy.

Latin: Tamarindus indica
Grow Zone: 10-11
Growth Rate: 1-3ft
Season: Early Summer
Height: 60ft
Fruit: 1-2, 6-8 Years

PROs
Nitrogen
Candy

CONs
Looks disgusting
Growing from seed takes a while

Avocado

One of America's favorite subtropical fruits. The unfortunate part is that they are very picky about where they grow. It has to be nice even temperatures year-round. No winter. No blazing summer. It can't be too humid. Avocados grow well, pretty exclusively to where they've always been grown. The American Southwest and Mexico. You can grow them in other places, but you will face some challenges.

Latin: Persea americana
Grow Zone: 9-11
Growth Rate: 2-3ft
Season: Summer-Fall
Height: 30ft
Fruit: 3-4 Years

PROs
Fats

CONs
Difficult to grow in other regions

Date Palm

I personally don't know why anyone would like dates, but they are ridiculously popular in certain parts of the world. Dates are one of the original sweeteners for the middle east and northern Africa. Dates are very sweet and full of sugars. Like most fruits they're still healthy, unlike refined sugar.

To grow date palms, you need a long hot summer. The soil cannot freeze. The tree is actually a shrub, meaning it won't have just one trunk, but several. For high quality fruit, it's always recommended to thin the fruit, regardless of the type of fruit. Date palms really need to be thinned. They produce so much fruit that the branches can snap.

Latin: Phoenix dactylifera
Grow Zone: 8-11
Growth Rate: 1ft
Season: Late Summer
Height: 60ft
Fruit: 4-8 Years

PROs
Produces a ton of fruit
Sweetener

CONs
Produces too much fruit
Gross

Mango

Have you ever had a garden tomato? It tastes totally different from those gross store tomatoes. Granted, that's true for most produce. I refuse to buy a grocery store watermelon ever again. Mangoes are one of those fruits that you need to buy locally, otherwise they'll be lame. I've never had a good mango. I don't live in the tropics, but I've heard that if you go to India, you need to try their mangoes, even if you think you don't like them.

The mango tree is easily grown from seed and is a very low effort tree. There are all sorts of varieties that ripen at different times of the year.

Latin: Mangifera indica
Grow Zone: 9-11
Growth Rate: 3-5ft
Season: Year-round
Height: 100ft
Fruit: 2-3 Years

PROs
India's top fruit
Year-round harvest

CONs
I've never liked it

Papaya

I don't know why, but for some reason my brain can't seem to figure out that papaya and mangoes are not the same fruit. They're not even from the same continent. Mango is the king of fruit for India. Papaya is the king for Central America, mainly Mexico. However, I almost left it off the list, because once again, I forgot they were different fruits.

The cool thing about papaya is that it doesn't have a season. Papaya fruits ripen at different times so you can harvest them all year round. You can also pick them when they're still green and eat them like a vegetable. You can also use the seeds as a spice, similar to black pepper.

Like mango, papaya is really easy to grow from seed, which is a good thing. Papaya trees don't live long. Commercially, farmers cut them down after four years and they typically only live seven years. Lucky for us, papaya starts fruiting after just one year, even if planted from seed. Papaya trees have weak roots, so they don't do good in windy locations.

Latin: Carica papaya
Grow Zone: 9-11
Growth Rate: 8ft
Season: Year-round
Height: 20ft
Fruit: 7-11 Months

PROs
Grows fast

CONs
Short life

Guava

Even though they aren't remotely related, think of guava as the tropical pear. The shape and texture of guava is often described as pear-like. The flavor is definitely tropical, but depending on the variety, it even has some slight pear notes too. Guava has two main colors and two main textures. There are crisp guavas and creamy guavas. There's also white guava and pink guava. All are considered tasty. I like guava juice, but I've never had fresh guava.

The guava tree is a true understory tropical plant. It likes heat, and water. You can grow it in the desert but you'll have to water it a ton. You can grow it in full sun, or dappled shade. I recommend shade. The tree will grow faster in the sun, more sun means more photosynthesis. However, the guava fruit is very susceptible to sunlight, and if the fruit gets too hot, it will actually ripen too fast. This will result in small and flavorless fruit.

Latin: Psidium
Grow Zone: 9-11
Growth Rate: 6-8ft
Season: Year-round
Height: 26ft
Fruit: 3-4 Years

PROs
Pear flavor

CONs
Lots of water

Olive

The humble olive tree. The source of one of the most consumed oils in the world. Unfortunately, it's also one of the most faked foods in the world. That said, let's debunk some myths. If you buy olive oil, it is almost certain that it is made from olives. However, if you're not in the mediterranean, it probably isn't extra virgin, made from fresh cold pressed olives. You have to buy expensive dark glass bottles with origin stickers, to even have a shot. The vast majority of "extra virgin" olive oil doesn't meet the international standards to be considered extra virgin, even if it does say so on the bottle. It's still olive oil, it's just not cold pressed extra virgin olive oil, which is where all the flavor and health benefits are.

Cold pressed means you take a fruit, in this case olives, and you place it into a press, squeezing all of the juices or oils out. You can increase the oil yield, by using chemicals, and heat, but this dramatically decreases the quality. You can also press the olives a second or third time to get a little extra out, or even use old rotting olives, but again this decreases the quality.

Extra virgin is just a quality standard. Virgin olive oil can't be produced with heat or chemicals. Extra virgin is the highest grade of virgin olive oil and has to meet specific chemical compounds and flavor tests to be extra virgin. Odds are, you've never actually tasted real extra virgin olive oil.

Now, is olive oil healthy? Yes. Is it any better for you than other historic sources of fats like tallow, lard, coconut, hickory, butter, etc? No! They're all plenty good for you. If your homestead is in an area where olives can grow, sure, grow an olive tree. If you're not, don't think you're missing out on this liquid gold.

As the olives mature from light green to dark, the more oil they contain, but they lose those flavors and compounds. So, you want to try and time your harvest to when the tree has both a lot of ripe olives and under ripe olives. Once harvested, you only have a few hours to press your olives into oil, before the quality starts to degrade.

Latin: Olea europaea
Grow Zone: 8-11
Growth Rate: Super Slow
Season: Fall
Height: 30 ft
Fruit: 3-5 Years

PROs
Oil

CONs
Faked

Starfruit

I've never tasted starfruit, but how it was described to me is that it has flavor notes of grape, mixed with citrus, and cinnamon, but is still very different from that. Starfruit comes in sweet and sour versions. It gets its name from the shape of the fruit. When you slice it, it slices into cute little stars. A lot of people will slice off the outer tips of the star, due to them being high in acid, but you don't have to.

The tree is a low maintenance tree. They like dappled shade, they hate the wind, but otherwise, they are easy to keep. Lastly, you don't have to wait for the fruit, the flowers are also edible.

Latin: Averrhoa carambola
Grow Zone: 9-11
Growth Rate: Fast
Season: Year-Round
Height: 30 ft
Fruit: 1-3 Years

PROs
Low maintenance
Little stars

CONs
Acid
Wind

Feijoa

Also known as pineapple guava, but not closely related to guava, this is a shrub. It tastes like pineapple, lemon, melon, guava, and kiwi all mixed together. You can eat it whole with the skin, or you can scoop out the sweet pulp, leaving behind the tart skin. Feijoa isn't ripe until after it falls to the ground, so don't pick it from the tree. You can also eat the flowers.

The tree is extremely drought tolerant but if you want fruit, it needs water. The tree is an evergreen myrtle that just happens to produce fruit.

Latin: Acca sellowiana
Grow Zone: 8-10
Growth Rate: Slow
Season: Late Fall
Height: 20ft
Fruit: 3 Years

PROs
Drought tolerant

CONs
Fruit needs lots of water

Lychee

The next three fruits are closely related. They're all soapberry trees. Think apricot vs. plum, or nectarine vs. peach. They're similar, but each is different. Flavor wise, lychee is like a tropical grape. The outside looks like a giant inedible raspberry. You eat the inside of the fruit, which is a translucent shiny white ball. It looks weird to me, kinda like an eyeball, but supposedly very tasty. Lychee trees are easily burned by too much nitrogen, so don't add too much, especially artificial nitrogen. Don't eat the seeds.

Latin: Litchi chinensis
Grow Zone: 9-11
Growth Rate: 1-2ft
Season: Summer
Height: 40ft
Fruit: 3-5 Years

PROs
Abundant fruit
Soap

CONs
Poisonous seeds

Longan

Longans are another soapberry fruit, similar to lychee. This one is brown on the outside. You can eat the longan shell, but typically you peel the shell to get access to white interior. This one looks even more like an eyeball. In fact, that's actually what longan means. It means dragon eye. They're a little less sweet than lychee, and have more of a mild melon flavor, but longan trees produce a ridiculous amount of fruit. Don't eat the seeds

Latin: Dimocarpus longan
Grow Zone: 8-11
Growth Rate: 2-3ft
Season: Late Summer
Height: 40ft
Fruit: 3-4 Years

PROs
Easy to peal
Lots of fruit
Soap

CONs
Poisonous seeds
Less sweet

Rambutan

This is a very weird looking fruit to me. The outside is a harry spikey mess. That's actually what rambutan means, harry fruit. Rambutans apparently have a little more flavor to them, with more tangy notes. The rambutan skin is the thickest out of the three and is usually cut with a knife. The cool thing about rambutan is that they have a short season, but they have two seasons, about six months apart. All three soapberry trees have a sap that can be used as soap. The three soapberry trees are lychee, longan, and rambutan. Rambutan is also the only one of the three whose seed can be eaten, but it first has to be roasted.

Latin: Nephelium lappaceum
Grow Zone: 10-12
Growth Rate: 2-3ft
Season: December, August
Height: 80ft
Fruit: 2-3 Years

PROs
Thick skin
Two harvests
Edible seeds
Soap

Mangosteen

Mangosteen is considered one of the best tasting fruits in the world. It has a thick outer casing that protects the white fleshy inside. It tastes like a combination of a grape, plum, and peach, but not exactly like them. To get to the fruit inside people typically use a knife to score the outer husk. Once inside, the fruit peels apart, similar to orange slices. Well, if it tastes so good, why isn't it more common? Mangosteen trees take up to 15 years to start producing. Good things come to those who wait, I guess.

Latin: Garcinia mangostana
Grow Zone: 11-12
Growth Rate: Slow
Season: Summer
Height: 80ft
Fruit: 15 Years

PROs
Delicious

CONs
Slow growing

Tamarillo

You know tomato is a fruit, right? The tamarillo is the cousin of the tomato and is called the tree tomato. Don't worry, it really only looks like a tomato. It's a tropical, sour, sweet, tangy fruit that is popular in South America. The cool thing about tamarillo trees is that they can be easily grown from seed and will start producing fruit in just 2 years. Unfortunately, it's not the strongest of trees. They don't like wind and they're not very drought tolerant. You'll want to prune this tree so that the fruit isn't growing on its weak branches, far away from the trunk.

Latin: Solanum betaceum
Grow Zone: 10-12
Growth Rate: Fast
Season: Early Summer - Fall
Height: 15ft
Fruit: 18-24 Months

PROs
Easy to grow

CONs
Weak branches
Drought

Soursop

Soursop gets its name because if you eat it too soon, it is unbelievably sour. When ripe, the soursop has a citrusy, strawberry, banana taste. It's like a fibrous sour apple. Don't eat it until it's nice and spongy. You don't want a hard soursop. Don't eat the seeds, and you can cut out the middle chunk. You then just take a spoon and scoop the fruit out. The leaves of the tree can be used to make an apparently tasty tea.

Latin: Annona muricata
Grow Zone: 1011
Growth Rate: 3ft
Season: Year-Round
Height: 25-30ft
Fruit: 3-5 Years

PROs
Lots of people's favorite fruit

CONs
Sour

Jackfruit

The biggest tree fruit in the world is the jackfruit. Think of a big melon, but growing on a tree. This massive fruit has a ton of uses. When picked green, it's used as a vegetable. If you let it grow to its maturity, it's a sweet fruit with a mixed taste of banana, pineapple, and mango. The seeds are pretty big too. They are roasted and consumed like nuts. Jackfruit is extremely sticky and it doesn't wash off with soap easily, but it does come off with oil.

Latin: Artocarpus heterophyllus
Grow Zone: 10-12
Growth Rate: 3-5ft
Season: Summer
Height: 70ft
Fruit: 3-4 Years

PROs
Massive
Nuts
Vegetable

CONs
Sticky

Breadfruit

Jackfruit and breadfruit are related. Breadfruit might actually be one of the more useful fruits in this chapter. Don't get me wrong, as a fruit, it's pretty lame. Think of bread fruit more like a starch crop than a fruit. Flavor wise, people describe it as a mix between a potato and bread. The fruit is roughly the size of a small loaf of bread. You have to bake it or roast it, and while you're roasting it, it smells like bread. It doesn't have as many calories as bread would, which calories are important when trying to live off the land, but it does have a lot of calories for a fruit.

Due to all of this, breadfruit is actually a staple crop and something you can use to feed your family. It also produces a latex substance on the outside husk that can be used as a water sealant for things like boats and tarps.

Latin: Artocarpus altilis
Grow Zone: 10-12
Growth Rate: 3-4ft
Season: Late Summer
Height: 70ft
Fruit: 2-5 Years

PROs
Staple crop

CONs
Not a "fruit"

Tropical Jujube

This is not the Chinese jujube that we talked about in the previous fruit chapter. This is the Indian or more commonly, the Thai jujube. The two trees are cousins and are so similar to each other, that even the experts mistake the two, but they are technically different trees. Again, the jujube is kinda like a mild apple taste, but is extra sweet like honey. The one thing that is different about the tropical version is that it's not consumed in different stages like the Chinese one. When the fruit gets too mature, it starts to get a little too dry tasting and airy.

Latin: Ziziphus mauritiana
Grow Zone: 10-12
Growth Rate: Extremely Fast
Season: Early Spring
Height: 45ft
Fruit: 3 Years

PROs
Sweet honey apple taste

CONs
Gets dry tasting

Black Sapote

This is an interesting fruit. It's cousin to the persimmon and that fruit is already unique enough for me. Like persimmons, you don't want to eat black sapote until it looks rotten and mushy. Now, persimmon is still orange and looks like a fruit at that stage. However, Black Sapote isn't good until it is black on the inside. Think of it texture wise, as chocolate pudding. Flavor wise, it tastes like pumpkin, which isn't surprising. Persimmons taste similar to pumpkin too.

Latin: Diospyros nigra
Grow Zone: 10-11
Growth Rate: Fast
Season: Late Fall
Height: 40ft
Fruit: 3-5 Years

PROs
Tropical version of persimmon

CONs
Looks rotten

CHAPTER 9
HOT CLIMATE NUTS

Again, nuts are fruits. Technically they're the seeds of fruits. Most of the nuts in temperate climates are obviously nuts. The fruit part, is an inedible thin husk. However, once we go down to the tropics, those lines get even more confusing. Jackfruit is a giant tropical fruit, with big fat seeds. Those seeds would be a nut. Brazil nuts are the seeds inside a big inedible fruit from the Brazilian rainforest. By the way, you can't grow a Brazil nut tree, so it's not included in this book. So, with that out of the way, lets dive in.

Cacao

Look, I know cacao isn't actually a nut. It's a fruit, but the only part of the cacao fruit that we care about are the hard crunchy seeds. We grind them up into a nutty powder and then mix with milk and sugar. So culinary wise, I'm counting it as a nut, and there's nothing you can do to stop me.

The cacao pod is this big husk that contains a lot of cacao beans. You crack it open, like a nut, and pull the beans out. At this stage they're slimy and coated in a white substance. You dry the beans out for a few weeks, and then grind them up, add sugar and milk, and now you have chocolate.

Latin: Theobroma cacao
Grow Zone: 11-13
Uses: Chocolate
Growth Rate: 2ft
Season: Oct-Mar
Height: 15-25ft
Fruit: 5 Years

PROs
Chocolate

CONs
Slime
Time consuming

Coconut

So a coconut actually is a nut, but we all know it's really a fruit. It's the ultimate survival fruit. Coconut water is extremely hydrating and full of electrolytes. The white flesh is full of calories and fats. The outer husk is great for starting a fire. The coconut shell makes for a decent water container. You can't boil water in the shell directly over a fire, but you can add hot rocks from the fire, to the coconut container. This will slowly bring the water up to a boil. To open a coconut you smack it around, and then there are three holes. There are the two eyes, and the mouth. Jab a stick into the mouth and pop it open.

Fun fact about the coconut, it is actually the most "invasive" plant in the world. No one hates that it was invasive because it's such a good tree, but coconut is the only "invasive" that colonized every region that it can possibly inhabit, without any human help. Coconuts float. They have that husk that helps them float around, and they're hollow inside. So, coconuts literally just floated across the oceans. They went from island to island, coast to coast, until they floated all the way across the globe.

Latin: Cocos nucifera
Grow Zone: 10-12
Uses: Fruit, water
Growth Rate: 2ft
Season: Year-round
Height: 80ft
Fruit: 6-10 Years

PROs
Super fruit
Coconut water

CONs
Tall trees

Cashew

The cashew is both a nut and a fruit. There's the cashew nut, but once it has formed, the cashew fruit starts to grow underneath the nut. They grow and mature together. You can eat the cashew fruit, but it's not very popular. There are no seeds in the cashew fruit because the nut on top of it, is the seed. You pick both together, and then you simply twist the nut off.

Cashews are expensive, not because they're hard to grow, but because you only get one small nut for every fruit and the shell is mildly toxic. Think super mild poison ivy. Processing a couple isn't bad, but processing a ton by hand damages the fingers.

Latin: Anacardium occidentale
Grow Zone: 10-11
Uses: Snack
Growth Rate: 3ft
Season: Early Spring
Height: 40ft
Fruit: 3 Years

PROs
A bonus fruit

CONs
Processing
Small nut

Macadamia

This one actually is a normal nut. They're expensive nuts due to the fact that the trees take 7 years to really start producing and they're relatively new to the world stage. Originally from Australia, the macadamia has been spread all across the tropics. The flowers are long, pink, pretty things. It's a low maintenance evergreen tree that is deer tolerant and drought tolerant. Good luck beating the squirrels to your nuts though. They swarm and devour everything.

Latin Macadamia integrifolia
Grow Zone: 9-11
Uses: Snack
Growth Rate: 2ft
Season: Summer
Height: 30-50ft
Fruit: 7-10 Years

PROs
Deer tolerant
Drought tolerant

CONs
7 years.
Squirrels

Breadnut

Also called Maya nut. Once again breadnut isn't actually a nut. It is the seeds from a fibrous fruit. You don't eat the fruit. Once it is soft enough to squish apart with your hands, you dig the seeds out. How breadnuts are typically consumed is pretty simple. You boil them, grind them up into a dough like paste, and then either bake them or fry them. Basically, you treat them like bread, hence the name. They're a carb heavy nut, similar to chestnuts, and they actually taste similar too. This tree was a staple to the Mayans and will provide you with a nice reliable source of calories. It looks like a little jackfruit, and that's because the two fruits are related and are part of the mulberry family. Oh, and like the mulberry tree, the leaves are used as fodder for livestock, especially in time of drought.

Latin: Brosimum alicastrum
Grow Zone: 10-12
Uses: Bread
Growth Rate: 2ft
Season: Year-round
Height: 100ft
Fruit: 3-5 Years

PROs
Carbs on a tree
Drought resistant
Fodder

Candlenut

This nut is grown all across the tropics, and yes, the nut can be used as a candle. Most nuts have a decent amount of fats in them, but candlenuts have just the right ratio of oil to sustain a small flame. Each nut will last about 15 minutes. Historically, people would string a thing of nuts together in order to maintain a small flame for hours. In Hawaii they named this practice kukui. The wood is also considered a premium wood. So much so that the people in Indonesia like to be buried in candlenut coffins.

You can of course eat the candlenut, and that's the main reason it's grown. The internet warns you not to eat them raw because they are mildly toxic, but they are popular both cooked and raw. Candlenuts are used in all sorts of curries, sauces, and as seasonings.

Latin: Aleurites moluccanus
Grow Zone: 10-12
Uses: Snack, light
Growth Rate: 2-5ft
Season: Year-round
Height: 20-50ft
Fruit: 4 Years

PROs
Snack
Light

CONs
Mildly toxic raw

Pistachio

This desert nut is probably my favorite nut. It's cold hardy enough that I almost stuck it in the other nut chapter, but it really is a hot desert nut. That said, most pistachios are grown in Iran, which is a relatively cool desert. As you might expect as desert plants, they are fairly drought tolerant. Pistachio trees naturally want to spread out horizontally, so if you want it to grow upright for easier harvesting, you have to prune and train the tree. When pistachios are ripe, they turn a nice red color and fall to the ground. How they are typically harvested is by laying a tarp on the ground and shaking the tree.

Latin: Pistacia vera
Grow Zone: 7-11
Uses: Snack
Growth Rate: 1-2ft
Season: Late Summer
Height: 20-30ft
Fruit: 8 Years

PROs
Best nut

CONs
Pruning
8 Years

CHAPTER 10
TROPICAL NITROGEN

You'll notice that there will be plenty of other nitrogen fixers in the next several chapters. These trees aren't necessarily better than those. The trees in this chapter have many uses, but the main reason they are planted is for their nitrogen fixing capabilities.

Pigeon Pea

Pigeon pea might be one of the more popular nitrogen fixers in the tropics. It produces pea pods that are a commonly consumed vegetable. You can eat them fresh, cook them, and even dry them for later. When dried, you can grind them into a flour similar to chickpea flour. If you're not interested in eating the peas, then you can always feed this incredible source of protein to your animals.

Latin: Cajanus cajan
Grow Zone: 9-12
Growth Rate: Fast
Height: 12ft
Nitrogen Fixer: Yes

PROs
Peapods
Nitrogen
Animal feed

River Tamarind

River tamarind is not the same thing as the fruit tamarind mentioned earlier. The pods are much flatter and smaller than their sweet-sour counterparts. If you want veggies, this is your tree. The young leaves, pods, and even the flowers are all consumed.

As you might guess, river tamarind is also a nitrogen fixer, but this version is a top dog. It's one of the best nitrogen fixers in the tropics.

It's originally from Mexico, but at this point, you can find it all across the tropical belt. That's because it's a popular plant to use for feeding livestock. Everything is edible. It's also used to prevent soil erosion. However, its most useful application is to shade and protect your crops from that harsh tropical sun.

Latin: Leucaena leucocephala
Grow Zone: 9-12
Growth Rate: Fast
Height: 40ft
Nitrogen Fixer: Yes

PROs
Nitrogen
Shade tree
Beans

Ice-cream Bean

The ice cream bean tree is exactly what it sounds like. It produces a bean pod that has this white fruit on the inside. It tastes and has a similar texture to that of ice cream. Different varieties have different minor flavors, but most people agree that it is similar to vanilla. The texture isn't quite like ice cream, it's more like a dense cotton candy. The main reason you'll want this tree is because of its beans, but it's also a good nitrogen fixer.

Latin: Inga edulis
Grow Zone: 9-11
Growth Rate: Fast
Height: 100ft
Nitrogen Fixer: Yes

PROs
"Ice-cream"
Nitrogen

Madre De Cacao

Also known as kakawate or gliricidia, madre de cacao means mother of chocolate. However, it's not remotely related to the cacao tree. Madre gets its name because it's a support plant. It's a nitrogen fixing shade tree that is planted to help cacao trees. That's why nitrogen fixers are awesome. Their job is to help other plants.

Now, you can plant more than just cacao trees underneath a madre de cacao, but historically madre was and is used as a support plant on cacao plantations. It fixes nitrogen, provides shade, has edible leaves and flowers. Heck, it's even an insect repellent, and can be used to treat bug bites as well as burns. Lastly, the flowers are pretty, so it's common to plant this tree as an ornamental.

Latin: Gliricidia sepium
Grow Zone: 10-12
Growth Rate: Fast
Height: 30-40ft
Nitrogen Fixer: Yes

PROs
Nitrogen
Shade
Edible
Insect repellant

Koa

Koa is the biggest Hawaiian tree. It's also one of the most expensive woods around. The most popular uses of the wood are for surfboards or ukuleles. Koa is an upland tree, but it can be grown in many locations.

Including this tree, the next several trees are all acacias, and acacias all make great nitrogen fixers.

Latin: Acacia koa
Grow Zone: 9-11
Growth Rate: 5ft
Height: 50-80ft
Nitrogen Fixer: Yes

PROs
Wood
Nitrogen

Golden Wattle

Australia's national flower. This is once again more of a large shrub than a true tree, but it's a cool nitrogen fixer so I'm tossing it in anyway. Australians used it for food, gum, and fibers. You can even make a treat out of it by soaking the gum in honey and water.

It gets the name wattle, because people used it to build homes. A wattle and daub home is built by weaving thin flexible sticks together, known as a wattle. You then stand your wattles up to create your walls. Daub is basically just clay and sand balls that you smear into the wattle to make an airtight home.

Like most wattle plants found in Australia, the golden wattle is a tough little bugger. Its seeds like to be burnt in wildfires. It doesn't require a lot of water, and it also grows back rapidly after you cut it. This is just what you want in a pioneering nitrogen fixer.

Wattles are a type of acacia and have a ton of flowers, but interestingly enough, they don't have any nectar.

Latin: Acacia pycnantha
Grow Zone: 9-11
Growth Rate: 3ft
Height: 26ft
Nitrogen Fixer: Yes

PROs
Flexable wood
Nitrogen
Flowers

CONs
No nectar

Tasmanian Blackwood

This tree originates in Tasmania, which is a southern state in Australia, but now it's grown all over. It's another type of acacia, and like most acacias, it's a pretty good nitrogen fixer. Most acacias are small pathetic little scrubby trees, but blackwood is a full-fledged timber tree.

Blackwood is considered a premium material for guitars. It's also popular for cabinets and for furniture like dining tables. It doesn't like to grow straight unless it's surrounded by competing plants, so don't plant this tree alone.

Woodworking is the main reason this tree is grown, but it has a few other cool aspects to it. The leaves were historically used as a makeshift soap, but people also used this leaf soap as a stunning agent for fishing. The bark was used to make string and is also a pain reliever. Oh, and speaking of leaves, you can use this tree as fodder for livestock. However, if you don't protect it when it's young it'll be eaten alive.

Latin: Acacia melanoxylon
Grow Zone: 8-11
Growth Rate: Fast
Height: 60ft
Nitrogen Fixer: Yes

PROs
Wood
Nitrogen
Livestock fodder

Tagasaste

Tagasaste has another name, its name is "Tree" Lucerne. Now, if you're an American like me, you probably haven't ever heard of the "plant" known as lucerne. If not, you'll know it by its other name, Alfalfa. Alfalfa is an incredible crop to grow for livestock. Tagasaste, like the black locust, has a very similar nutrient profile to that of alfalfa. The difference is it's for hot dry climates, namely our friends down under. Tagasaste comes from Australia and is used to multiply the land's ability to feed livestock. It's an evergreen shrub full of high protein leaves.

If you're wanting to use it for livestock, your goal is to try and keep it from flowering. The reason why is because once it flowers, the leaves get gross. However, if you have bees, they love tagasaste flowers.

Oh, and did I mention it's also a nitrogen fixer? Like most nitrogen fixers it is a pretty aggressive tree and will need to be pruned to keep it from overrunning your pasture. Luckily, when you do trim it, it will be releasing nitrogen into the surrounding soil, feeding the grass.

Latin: Cytisus proliferus
Grow Zone: 8-12
Growth Rate: Fast
Height: 12ft
Nitrogen Fixer: Yes

PROs
Protein
Nitrogen

CHAPTER 11
TROPICAL TREES

Hot. Hot. Hot. What's the weather like down there? Hot. If you live somewhere winter doesn't exist, the trees in this chapter will like you. Technically most desert trees could be included in this chapter, but since the desert is its own beast, I went ahead and gave it its own chapter.

The Miracle Tree

Moringa, the miracle tree. Moringa is the one tropical tree that is so awesome I still want to grow it in cooler climates. I guess there's citrus too, but that's a given. It's native to hot, dry regions but it's also grown in the sub-tropics and the tropical belt. Think of moringa as nature's multivitamin. The tree's roots extract such an abundant amount of nutrients from deep within the soil that the nutrient profile of the leaves is off the charts. Every part of the tree is edible and useful. The roots can be used for tea. The juices in the bark are used to heal wounds. The leaves and pods are eaten as food. The seeds are incredible too. They can be eaten when still green. However, when ripe, they are full of oil that you can press and use for cooking or for cosmetic purposes, including sunburns. The press cake, the leftover gunk, is used to purify dirty water. It's kind of like purification tablets, but not really. Moringa is a natural coagulant and flocculant. Basically, it pulls the bad microbes and dirt out of the water and makes it all sink to the bottom.

Now, moringa is a desert/tropical tree, but it grows super-fast and it's easy to grow from seed. What we're after is the leaves. This means that we northerners with this nasty thing called winter, can still grow it as an annual. Unfortunately, if you want to collect seeds, you'll have to protect at least one tree over the winter.

Latin: Moringa oleifera
Grow Zone: 9-10
Growth Rate: 10ft
Height: 40ft
Nitrogen Fixer: No

PROs
Vitamins
Fodder
Water purification

Eucalyptus

Eucalyptus is an entire family of trees that are native to and that dominate the Australian landscape. As the tree gets older, the leaves droop so they don't get hit by too much solar radiation. The oil is abundant on purpose. Having oil present in the tree makes it burn faster. A fast burn keeps the roots of the tree alive. Even though they love water, if drought hits, they'll just cut off a limb or a branch and let it die. Don't park your car underneath.

Eucalyptus, specifically blue gum eucalyptus, was brought to America because it's a fast-growing tree that grows straight, and its oil is a natural insect repellent. The idea was to use it as a timber tree. One problem, the wood warps so badly that it's unusable as timber. However, it's one of the hottest burning firewoods in the world. Unfortunately, it only grows in warm regions. The medicinal properties of the oil are pretty sweet too. It's a respiratory oil that helps the lungs, clears mucus, eases coughs, and when inhaled, it eases pain.

Latin: Eucalyptus
Grow Zone: 8-11
Growth Rate: 6-10ft
Height: 180ft
Nitrogen Fixer: No

PROs
Medicinal
Firewood
Drought resistant

CONs
Warping

Rubber Tree

Modern rubber is synthetic and is derived from petroleum, but historically one of the most important trees was the rubber tree. This tree produces a ton of latex in its sap. Latex is what rubber is made from.

Now, the harvesting process is pretty simple. It's not quite the same, but it's similar to tapping maple trees for syrup. Little grooves are cut in the tree, and then the sap drips down a tap into a bucket. The rubber sap will naturally coagulate until you have a small ball of rubber and some leftover liquid.

If you don't know how important and useful rubber is, I suggest you do some additional research, but let me give you one example. On the homestead you probably want some animals, but if not, you still have yourself. At the very least, your pumps and plumbing have rubber gaskets. A pressure tank uses rubber to supply you with stable water pressure. If you have some flexible hose or tubing, it probably is made of rubber. For now, you can just buy these things, but if you're in the tropics, maybe plant a rubber tree just to be safe.

Latin: Hevea brasiliensis
Grow Zone: 10-12
Growth Rate: 2ft
Height: 130ft
Nitrogen Fixer: No

PROs
Rubber

CONs
No longer commercially viable

Bay

The tree is known as bay laurel, but we all know it as those random leaves you have tucked away in the back of your spice cabinet. The bay laurel is from the Mediterranean and likes hot temperatures, but likes to be protected from the afternoon sun. Bay leaves are used in soups to create a subtle flavor that can be hard to notice in more complex recipes. However, in simple meals like tomato soup, it adds a nice subtle flavor. Medicinally, bay leaves can help with joint pain.

Latin: Laurous nobilus
Grow Zone: 8-11
Growth Rate: 1ft
Height: 60ft
Nitrogen Fixer: No

PROs
Soup

All Spice

This is a tropical tree that is popular all across the world, but it truly dominates Caribbean cuisine. The parts we call allspice are the dried berries, which are ground up into a powder. In American cuisine, it's mainly used in ketchup and pumpkin pie. The reason why it's called allspice is because it tastes like a combination of pepper, nutmeg, clove, ginger, and cinnamon.

The allspice tree is a beautiful evergreen tree that has shiny green leaves that smell good. The leaves, when dried, look similar to bay leaves and can be used in soups and stews. In fact, the two trees are cousins.

Latin: Pimenta dioica
Grow Zone: 10-12
Growth Rate: 2ft
Height: 60ft
Nitrogen Fixer: No

PROs
Ketchup
Soup
Spices

Oil Palm

The oil palm tree is the single greatest oil crop that the world has access to, and it's not even close. No plant provides us with more cooking oil than the oil palm. It only takes 4 years for it to start producing, and it produces more oil than any other plant.

Palm oil is in everything. It's the most consumed oil in food and the most utilized grease in cosmetics. Some political groups hate the oil palm tree because of rainforest deforestation, but what's the alternative? A crop that takes 10x the land? If your homestead is in the tropical belt, oil palm is the best choice of plant oil.

The oil palm tree produces big bunches of fruit. This fruit is full of oil. Once ripe, you separate the fruit and boil it to soften it up. Then it's a simple process of grinding, smashing it up, and watching the oil flow out. The seed is also used for oil, but that's mainly used in industrial settings and is for cosmetics.

Palm oil can be refined to be tasteless, but in its normal state it has a strong flavor. Not a bad flavor; it has a spice to it. Coconut oil has a strong flavor too, it tastes like coconut. Palm oil tastes like palm oil. Similar to coconut oil, and unlike every other plant oil, palm oil is very shelf stable and doesn't go rancid quickly.

Latin: Elaeis guineensis
Grow Zone: 10-12
Harvest Rate: 4 Years
Height: 65ft
Nitrogen Fixer: No

PROs
Cooking oil

CONs
Deforestation

Neem

Neem trees grow incredibly fast and produce a ton of biomass. The leaves and the fruit are what everyone is after. If you've heard of neem, it's probably because the oil (derived from the seeds and fruit) is an incredible pest and fungus control for your garden. You don't have to buy the oil. A bucket of water filled with leaves from your neem tree will still do the trick, but it's not quite as effective. Speaking of water and leaves, neem tea is actually a common medicinal drink. In India, neem is one of the most commonly used ayurvedic herbs, and it's known as a heal all. It's used for everything from sickness to skincare.

Latin: Azadirachta indica
Grow Zone: 10-12
Growth Rate: 4-8ft
Height: 75ft
Nitrogen Fixer: No

PROs
Insecticide
Medicinal

Ylang Ylang

This name is just a fun name to say "e-lang e-lang". Ylang is a perfume flower tree used in a ton of the top perfumes. The most notable is Chanel-No.5. The flowers are harvested in the early pre-dawn and then processed and distilled into an oil. As a tree, it's just a sweet smelling, pretty tree. If you don't pick the flowers, it will produce a small tart fruit that is edible. You can grind up the flowers and use it for skin health, bug bites, and dandruff. The oil is used for mood boosting, stress, and as an aphrodisiac. However, the most important use of this oil is to treat malaria—one of the top killers of humanity.

Latin: Cananga odorata
Grow Zone: 9-11
Growth Rate: 5-10ft
Height: 60ft
Nitrogen Fixer: No

PROs
Malaria treatment
Perfume
Skin health
Bug bites
Dandruff
Mood boosting
Aphrodisiac

Lemon Myrtle

Lemon myrtle is a culinary tree with pretty white flowers. Known for its strong lemon scent and flavor, lemon myrtle is used as a flavoring agent and as a tea. The tea is very popular just for its taste, but it's also medicinal. It'll soothe a sore throat. Applied topically, lemon myrtle oils are good for skin issues.

You can dry the leaves and grind them into a seasoning powder. Lemon myrtle seasoning is popular on fish, chicken, and even alligator. If you like homemade yogurt, you can toss some leaves in to give it a lemony flavor.

Latin: Backhousia citriodora
Grow Zone: 9-11
Growth Rate: Slow
Height: 20ft
Nitrogen Fixer: No

PROs
Tasty
Sore throats

Sapodilla

Sapodilla is a fruit tree, but I went ahead and stuck it in this chapter because the main reason you'd want this tree is actually for its gummy sap. We already talked about the mastic tree, the gumtree of the Mediterranean. In a couple of chapters we'll talk about the real source of chewing gum. However, if you want a tropical source of chewing gum, the sap of sapodilla was the chewing gum of the Mayans. The catch is, you can only harvest the sap every 14 years.

Oh, and similar to persimmons, you'll want to eat this fruit once it's overripe and mushy. It has a rich sweet taste similar to molasses. Do not eat the sharp seeds.

Latin: Manilkara zapota
Grow Zone: 10-11
Growth Rate: Slow
Height: 100ft
Nitrogen Fixer: No

PROs
Chewing gum
Fruit

CONs
14 Year cycle

Sandalwood

Money! Sandalwood oil is a very expensive product, primarily because of its potent fragrance, which comes from the heartwood of a mature sandalwood tree. Trees take a while to grow. This makes supply small. Large demand, small supply means it is a very profitable tree. That said, because we're after the oil, not the timber, it's actually a short rotation of only 15 years. That sounds like a long time, but I planted black walnuts for profit, and that takes a minimum of 30 years. The trees are very hardy and great in a silvopasture or for a forest cropping setup.

Now there are some medicinal benefits to sandalwood oil; mostly skin, hair, and mood. But the truth is there are other cheaper oils out there that do a better job. Sandalwood oil is prized because it smells so freaking good.

Latin: Santalum
Grow Zone: 10-11
Growth Rate: 5ft
Height: 30ft
Nitrogen Fixer: No

PROs
Money
Perfume
Medicinal
15 year cycle

Tamanu

Tamanu is a tropical island tree that is grown for oil. It's a cosmetic oil and is used for anything skin related. It can be used for beauty things like stretch marks, wrinkles, and acne. It's also apparently used for major medical issues like rashes and infections. Tamanu leaves can be used to make a tea for eye infections. The oil is also good for the hair.

Latin: Calophyllum inophyllum
Grow Zone: 10-12
Growth Rate: Slow
Height: 65ft
Nitrogen Fixer: No

PROs
Skin care

Tung Nut

Tung nut trees were planted for their nuts. The nuts were prized not for eating, but for wood. Tung oil is a historical finishing oil for woodworking, and is considered far superior to linseed. Historic finishers aren't very popular these days because you do have to reapply the finish every few months. Even modern cans of tung oil only contain a small amount and are full of more modern ingredients to make it last longer. That said, traditional (or pure tung oil) is still a high-quality finish that you can make yourself.

Latin: Vernicia fordii
Grow Zone: 8-11
Harvest Rate: 3-4 Years
Height: 40ft
Nitrogen Fixer: No

PROs
Finishing oil

CONs
Not permanent

Spinach Tree

Spinach is a northern cold weather plant. Chaya, also known as the spinach tree, is a very popular tropical tree. Unfortunately, chaya leaves can only be eaten when cooked, and can't be cooked in an aluminum pot. They will have a chemical reaction with each other, that if consumed will give you diarrhea. Also, depending on the variety it can have stinging thorns on the back, similar to stinging nettle. Don't let that scare you off. It was a staple crop for the Mayans for a reason.

Latin: Cnidoscolus aconitifolius
Grow Zone: 8-11
Harvest Rate: 6 months
Height: 9ft
Nitrogen Fixer: No

PROs
Food

CONs
Stingers
Has to be cooked

Mahogany

On my homestead I planted black walnuts. When I'm old and gray, hopefully it'll give me a nice influx of cash. If I were in the tropics, I would have planted mahogany. Mahogany is a valuable wood that grows straight and is easy to maintain. It likes hot, humid air and sandy soil. If that sounds like your environment, I recommend you plant this tree as a retirement tree. Fun fact, it has these big pods that release cool little helicopter seeds.

Latin: Swietenia macrophylla
Grow Zone: 10-11
Growth Rate: 2-3ft
Height: 60ft
Nitrogen Fixer: No

PROs
Money

Teak

The other tropical wood tree that I might recommend you plant is teak. A teak tree is usually lumber ready in about 20 years and is the go-to wood for luxury products like yachts, decks, saunas, sailboats, etc. That's because it's easy to shape and the wood has oils that protect it from termites and wet conditions.

Latin: Tectona grandis
Grow Zone: 10-12
Growth Rate: 6-9ft
Height: 150ft
Nitrogen Fixer: No

PROs
Handles wet conditions
20 Year Cycle

CHAPTER 12
DESERT TREES

So, I know cold deserts exist. In fact, I wrote most of this book in a frozen wasteland… also known as northern Utah. But the vast majority of deserts are in hot regions, and the truth is that cold deserts don't have a lot of trees. Brush is what dominates the landscape in those regions. That said, I know lots of people live in cold deserts like Idaho, Utah, and Iran. So real quick, your top fruits would be apricots, pears, and nectarines. Russian olive is an aggressive nitrogen fixer. Cottonwood is the main historical source of firewood. All are trees I covered in previous chapters. There are also many trees that can grow in cold, dry regions that will be included in the cold chapter. That really only leaves a handful of hot desert trees, so this chapter won't be that long. Now, the good news is that with just a little bit of irrigation, you can grow a lot of other trees too. Utah and Arizona have a ton of orchards.

Mesquite

If there is one desert tree that could be crowned the king of desert trees it would be mesquite. Even if you've never lived in a dry environment, you've probably heard of mesquite. The main reason you'd know of this tree is because of BBQ. Mesquite is a common flavor enhancer, and you know the flavor. It's the taste of Texas barbecue. People use mesquite for seasoning, and its wood to smoke meat.

The most important part of a mesquite tree is its bean pods. The pods of mesquite were and are a staple food crop. In the American Southwest, it was a major part of people's diets. Basically, you grind the beans and pods into a flour and then use it like… flour. Nowadays, people will usually mix mesquite flour with wheat flour, but historically you would make little mesquite cakes by the fire. Texas honey mesquite is considered by far the best-tasting variety. I'd take a guess and say that's why mesquite is more common in Texan cuisine, but the other varieties of mesquite are still considered a good source of desert food.

Here's the interesting thing about mesquite pods. The bean is where all the calories and nutrients are, but the pod itself is where all the flavor is. So when you grind them up, grind the whole thing. In fact, the beans are actually higher in protein than soy. When you harvest, do not harvest from the ground. There is an invisible fungus that will grow on the fallen pods. It will make you incredibly sick. Only harvest the pods from the tree, and do it before monsoon season. The pods are ready when you can snap them in half. If they're not dry enough to snap, then they will gum up the flour mill.

Alright, enough about the beans. The wood is rot-resistant and is used for fence posts. The sap has been used for treating fungus issues and can be applied to wounds. Finally, mesquite is a really good nitrogen fixer, and its leaf litter is full of nitrogen. This creates a nitrogen mound. Basically, the dirt around the mesquite tree becomes quality soil and as it fills up with other plant life, it creates a small mound above the rest of the desolate desert dirt.

Latin: Prosopis
Grow Zone: 6-9
Growth Rate: 2-3ft
Height: 50ft
Nitrogen Fixer: Yes

PROs
Nitrogen
Beans
BBQ
Smokin

CONs
Invisible fungus

Palo Verde

Palo verde literally means "green stick." This is the state tree of Arizona and is the ultimate drought-tolerant tree. You see, photosynthesis is how plants turn sunlight into food. This is usually done through leaves. No leaves, no photosynthesis. However, the bigger the leaf, the more water the tree needs to keep the leaf alive. The palo verde tree has a bunch of tiny leaves, but that's not its secret. During times of drought, palo verde just drops its leaves. This creates a problem cause it still needs to grow. That's where the name comes in. The bark of the palo verde tree is green and is actually almost as good at photosynthesis as its leaves. This allows it to keep growing even when there's no water available for leaves.

That's cool and all, but why is this one of the most useful trees in the desert? Well, it's a nitrogen fixer. That's especially important in the desert. It also provides a nice dappled shade which protects the plants under it from that harsh desert sun. Finally, it has edible bean pods. They can be eaten young and fresh like peas, or you can harvest them when dried and use them as a dry bean. Like mesquite, only harvest the beans from the tree, not the ground. The beans contain 32% protein, so even if you're not interested in eating them, they still make great fodder.

It's also a really popular ornamental. In desert environments it grows better than most trees, so it's planted a lot. It's a pretty tree year-round and provides shade, but in the spring, it has a ton of edible and gorgeous yellow flowers. Unfortunately, it also has thorns, and the wood is completely unusable for firewood. It's full of foul-smelling compounds that can cause allergic reactions when inhaled. It's also a weak tree and breaks in strong winds.

Latin: Parkinsonia aculeata
Grow Zone: 8-11
Growth Rate: 1-2ft
Height: 20ft
Nitrogen Fixer: Yes

PROs
Nitrogen
Shade
Drought resistant
Beans
Fodder
Flowers

CONs
Thorns
Do not burn

Desert Ironwood

This is the third king of the desert. The desert ironwood is the tree of the Sonoran Desert. It is originally only from the Sonoran Desert and is found throughout 100% of the entire Sonoran Desert. It is one of the three keystone species of the American Southwest. The others are paleo verde and mesquite. Hence why I called it the third king. Like the other two, it's also a nitrogen fixer, but due to its slow growth, I would say it's probably not a good one.

It produces a bean you can eat, but you'll want to boil them to remove the tannins and then roast them. Once roasted, they taste similar to peanuts.

The tree is a small scrubby desert tree, but it is tough. It's the eighth densest wood in the world and seriously, look up what ironwood looks like. It is gorgeous. Due to its size, you really only see the wood used in small things like knife handles. It's also not the easiest to work with because it is so tough. However, once done, it's pretty and solid as iron.

Now back to the tree itself. It's evergreen with pretty violet and white flowers. The little leaves don't require much water and they provide protective shade for lots of plants underneath.

Latin: Olneya tesota
Grow Zone: 9-11
Growth Rate: 1ft
Height: 30ft
Nitrogen Fixer: Yes

PROs
Penut like beans
Tough, gorgeous wood.

CONs
Slow growing
Small

Argan

This desert evergreen is a popular ornamental, but it also produces one of the most expensive cosmetic oils. Argon produces a fruit with a lot of oil-rich seeds. Moroccans figured out that the oil has a lot of benefits. Basically, argan oil is like tamanu, a catch-all for anything skin-related. You can use it for simple beauty things like stretch marks, wrinkles, and acne. You can use it for major medical issues like rashes and infections. I don't know how effective it is compared to cheap, easily accessible oils and medicines, but that is what it's used for.

Here's the catch, the tree is a thorny nightmare. It also takes forever to grow. It's an easy tree to maintain, but it takes 15-20 years to start producing fruit. This is why the oil is so expensive.

Moroccan goats, fattened on argan fruit, are a popular food. It's popular because they use goats to harvest the fruit and then collect the seeds from the poop

Latin: Argania spinosa
Grow Zone: 9-11
Harvest Rate: 15-20 Years
Height: 25ft
Nitrogen Fixer: No

PROs
Skin health
Goat food

CONs
Thorny nightmare
15-20 Years

Curry Tree

By the name, you might guess that this tree is used to make curry powder, but that's wrong. Curry powder is a spice mix that was invented in Britain, to replicate Indian cuisine. Curry is just a type of South Asian soup, and curry leaves are often used as a flavor enhancer in some curry soups. It's similar to how bay leaves are used in Western soups. Speaking of, I wonder what a curry leaf tomato soup would taste like.

You harvest the leaves by trimming the tree. You can either use them fresh or dry them and grind them into a powder. The best thing about this tree is that it's considered a weedy tree. A.K.A., it's super easy to grow. The leaves, ground into a paste, are used for burns. The seeds are not edible. Oh, and the tree smells great.

Latin: Bergera koenigii
Grow Zone: 9-12
Growth Rate: 1-2ft
Height: 15ft
Nitrogen Fixer: Yes

PROs
Seasoning
Easy to grow
Burn ointment

Carob

This tree comes from the Mediterranean & Middle East. It handles drought well. It grows extremely slow. It's a pretty evergreen, with little dark green leaves. However, the reason why you want it is for its bean pods. The seeds are hard as a rock, but the pod is chewy. It's described as candy on a tree. It's a very sweet fruit and can be eaten fresh or turned into carob molasses/syrup. The flavor is supposed to be similar to chocolate. It also has a ton of potassium.

Latin: Ceratonia siliqua
Grow Zone: 9-11
Harvest Rate: 6-7 Years
Height: 50ft
Nitrogen Fixer: Yes

PROs
Candy
Syrup

Jamun

Jamun, also known as java plum, is a fruit tree from India. Well, if it's a fruit tree, why is it in the desert chapter and not in the tropical fruit chapter? Easy, that chapter is long, this one is short. However, I'm justifying it because this is also a fast-growing shade tree that loves the sun, even in the desert. It's two for one. You get a fruit tree that can also provide protective shade for more fruit trees.

Texture-wise, it's similar to a grape, but the fruit is mildly astringent and doesn't taste anything like a grape. The tree also has a deep tap root which helps it during dry periods, but this means it doesn't grow well in a pot.

Latin: Syzygium cumini
Grow Zone: 10-11
Harvest Rate: 4-10 Years
Height: 40ft
Nitrogen Fixer: Yes

PROs
Fruit
Shade
Deep tap root

Jojoba

The oil plant that failed. Back in the 80's, jojoba was supposed to be "the big new oil crop." The crop wasn't understood at the time, so most jojoba farms failed. Basically, the farms ended up with way too many male trees and not enough females. That said, it's still pretty useful. It's a great oil crop and a nut tree. You can eat the nuts. They're an appetite suppressant and they taste kind of like a bitter almond. The oil is primarily used for cosmetics. It's hydrating, helps with acne, soothes sunburns, and helps with hair growth and dandruff. You can also use it for fuel in an oil lamp or heater.

Latin: Simmondsia chinensis
Grow Zone: 8-11
Harvest Rate: 3-4 Years
Height: 10ft
Nitrogen Fixer: Yes

PROs
Oil crop
Nuts
Skin health
Appetite suppressant
Fuel

CONs
Polination issues

CHAPTER 13
COLD CLIMATE TREES

I already know what my frozen snow bunnies are going to say. "But this tree only goes down to Zone 5." Well, my crazy friends, for some reason y'all want to flex about who can endure the most stupid levels of cold. If your winter lasts the majority of the year, I hate to break it to you but you live in a frozen hellscape. I've lived in many a frozen hellscape over the years, and can understand the appeal... doesn't mean our tropical friends are wrong for calling Zone 6 cold.

The most notable cold tree that is not in this chapter is pine, and that's because it's so useful we already talked about it. There are also countless trees in other chapters that can be grown in climates much colder than Zone 5. The purpose of this chapter is just to clean up the leftover trees that are specifically useful, and/or dominant, in cold climates.

So quick definitions. Most of the trees found in the frigid north are conifers. There's a science-y definition, but just think of trees with needles, like pine needles. Deciduous means the tree loses its leaves in the fall. Evergreen means the leaves stay green all year. Most non-tropical trees are deciduous, with the exception being that most conifers are evergreen. There are a few exceptions to these, including the first tree in this chapter.

Larch

The king of the cold is the larch. The American larch is known as "tamarack." Tamarack likes low wet areas. Alpine larch can live high up the mountains. They live above the normal tree line. Western larch can survive extreme fires. There are also European and Japanese larches, and they're the ones used most commonly for ornamental purposes.

Larch is a conifer. Most conifers are evergreen, meaning the needles stay on the tree year-round. Larch is not an evergreen. It turns yellow in the fall and drops all of its needles. Most conifers keep their needles so they can get more sun in long winters. Larch is built different. It handles such cold weather that it decided the tradeoff was worth it. No needles, less heavy snow on the branches. Larch is the hardwood for the extreme cold. It's not as durable as something like white oak or maple, and it doesn't grow as fast as pine or fir, but tamarack specifically grows faster than the other cold hardwoods and has way more durability than the softwoods. Also, it's really pretty in the fall. Oh, and larches live for a thousand years, which is just cool.

Latin: Larix
Grow Zone: 2-6
Growth Rate: 2ft
Height: 60-80ft
Nitrogen Fixer: No

PROs
Stronger than softwoods
Faster than hardwoods
Pretty fall colors
Extreme colds

Ash

The humble ash tree, considered one of the best hardwoods in the northern hemisphere. The tree grows straight and fast. The wood is strong and flexible. It steam bends really well, so it is popular for building furniture. Historically, the strong, flexible poles were important for making spears and building roofs for huts.

There's a lot of mythos involved with this tree due to its importance, especially in Norse myths. The bark can be used to treat skin ailments. The leaves are an important source of feed for livestock. The wood is a good burning log, and is excellent for smoking meat.

Unfortunately, the North American ash trees are critically endangered. They used to be everywhere in our forests and were a very popular ornamental tree. They have lots of pretty fall colors. But then one day, a beetle known as the emerald ash borer hitched a ride on some lumber from China. This beetle is considered one of the most invasive bugs on the planet. Once it made a home in America, it spread like wildfire and has decimated most of the ash trees here. Chinese ash trees can handle its presence, but American ash trees can't. Currently, the only way to keep an American ash protected from the beetle is through a large amount of pesticides.

Latin: Fraxinus
Grow Zone: 3-9
Growth Rate: 1-2ft
Height: 35-75ft
Nitrogen Fixer: No

PROs
Strong & flexible
Steam bending
Livestock fodder
Smoking meat

Fir

The Christmas tree. Technically all conifers are used as Christmas trees but the main one is fir trees. Most homes In North America are built using fir, pine, or spruce. They're all excellent timber trees. The bark of the balsam fir is prized for its oil. Balsam fir oil is used for sore muscles, respiratory issues, and for the skin. The needles of the Siberian fir are used to make oils. Siberian fir oil is soothing. It soothes you mentally, and it soothes sore aching muscles, so it's popular in massages. Heck, fir needles in general are just a really healthy source of nutrients.

Fir trees have these little bumps on their trunks that are full of resin. You can pop the blister and use this resin for wounds, sores, and bites. It has a healing effect and will protect them from possible infections. It's also very flammable, which is useful in a survival situation. Speaking of survival, you can eat the inner bark.

Latin: Abies
Grow Zone: 4-7
Growth Rate: 1-2ft
Height: 60-90ft
Nitrogen Fixer: No

PROs
Christmas
Home building
Medicinal oil
Edible bark

Douglas Fir

So douglas fir isn't technically a fir. They're so similar that I don't know why scientists felt the need to make it its own family of one. Its Latin name includes pseudo, which is funny because that literally just means fake. Like true fir trees, douglas fir is an excellent timber tree. It's also very medicinal. Once again, just like true firs, the resin is good, needles are good, the inner bark is edible. The oil for douglas fir is extracted from the needles and is used for lungs, colds, and is used topically for skin care. Unlike most conifers, mushrooms are actually quite fond of douglas fir, and so its logs can be used as mushroom logs. Oh, and remember how fir trees are Christmas trees? The vast majority are douglas fir. (Poor douglas, I don't know why it got exiled from the fir family)

So, redwoods are the biggest trees in the world, but douglas firs can rival them. In fact, the tallest tree ever recorded was a douglas fir back in the 1890s at an insane 465 ft. tall. This was a verifiable and reliable recording, which is interesting. You see, according to theoretical scientists, the limit a tree can grow is 425 ft. This 465 ft douglas isn't the only tree to have passed this limit, but it was the biggest. The current champ is a redwood at 380 ft.

Latin: Pseudotsuga menziesii
Grow Zone: 4-6
Growth Rate: 1-2ft
Height: 250ft
Nitrogen Fixer: No

PROs
Christmas
Edible bark
Mushrooms

CONs
It's the ugly exiled step child

Poplar

Cottonwoods, aspens, and willows are all poplars, but in this section, I'm specifically talking about the trees known as "poplars." This excludes the tulip poplar, which we already talked about and isn't related.

The two most notable poplars are the hybrid poplar and the Lombardy poplar. Lombardy is mostly used as a windbreak, which is something very important up north. The hybrid poplar is the offspring of the North African black poplar and the American cottonwood. It's incredibly fast growing and is perfect for a shade tree. Due to its fast growth, it is grown on plantations as a source for pulpwood. Pulpwood is used to make paper. You specifically can use these trees as fast-growing fodder crops. Poplar leaves are a good source of feed for livestock. Also, the inner bark is used medicinally to aid the kidneys.

Latin: Populus
Grow Zone: 3-9
Growth Rate: 5-8ft
Height: 70ft
Nitrogen Fixer: No

PROs
Shade
Windbreak
Livestock fodder
Medicinal

CONs
Weak wood

Spruce

The other main Christmas tree is the spruce. I'm used to the blue spruce, but all the other spruces are a nice green color. The first thing I learned about spruce is that in the spring time you can snack on the lighter colored new growth tips. I've done that a few times over the years. It tastes fine. You can also boil the needles of any age to make a vitamin rich tea. The small, young, male cones are also edible early in the spring.

Now let's talk about its main foraging advantage: chewing gum. We've talked about chewing gum trees in other chapters, but this is the real one. Spruce gum, flavored with mint, is why there's a strong bubblegum industry in modern times. Spruce gum is also the easiest to produce. It's abundant and you can literally just pick the resin off of the tree and start chewing it. Now typically you'll want to purify and flavor it, but that's not hard. There are videos that explain it more but I'll cover it real quick. You can boil or render the resin in an oven. You then just strain the goop. Now you have this liquid resin. This is when you'll want to add flavors like mint. Once that resin starts to solidify, you'll want to mold it like play dough into a long string and cut the string up into bite sized pieces. That's it.

Unlike modern gum, this gum/resin is medicinal. It is great for oral health and it is antimicrobial. Now after all of that work, you probably want to chew the purified gum, so let's backtrack to plain resin. It is great for wounds. The resin is soothing and has healing properties, so people use it for a bunch of stuff like boils, cysts, and even acne.

Oh, and back to purifying the resin. Once you've strained the liquid resin out, you have all the leftover solid, waxy resin. I used the term waxy on purpose. You can use that stuff to make a nice smelling spruce candle. In a survival situation, you can use spruce resin to make a decent torch. Oh, and speaking of survival, spruce roots can be used for cordage.

Latin: Picea
Grow Zone: 2-7
Growth Rate: 1-3ft
Height: 60-90ft
Nitrogen Fixer: No

PROs
Edible
Chewing gum
Wax

Pasific Madrone

Here's another tree that didn't stick to the boxes we want to put things in. This tree looks like it belongs in a tropical rainforest. It has bright red bark that flakes off, revealing a green under bark. It has these large, velvety green leaves that grow year-round. It has lovely flowers and little red berries... It's also considered a native in Canada. Now to be fair, it has a long range. It goes from Canada all the way to Mexico, and most of its cousins are native to mediterranean and subtropical regions. And truthfully, it shouldn't be in this chapter, but still. It looks like it belongs in a tropical rainforest and yet it can be grown on a mountain in Canada. So, I'm sticking it here.

In fact, speaking of mountains, madrone loves rocky terrain. The pacific madrone tree is considered the king of the strawberry trees. Strawberry trees are a family of trees that like to grow out of cliffs. They all produce an edible and pretty fruit, that by all accounts is at best, meh. Madrone fruit historically was boiled and the juices were used to flavor water. In the spring the flowers are lovely and smell like lilacs. Hummingbirds love them.

The madrone tree not only is fire tolerant, it's kinda built for it. It's happy with water, it's happy with drought, but it loves fire. Madrones are an opportunistic tree. When fires burn the forest down, they spring into action. They quickly regrow from roots and the fire-scorched seeds start sprouting. Once the tree is old, it'll put on a thicker bark to protect it, but while it's young it's happy to be burnt. Oh and speaking of fire, madrone is considered a top dog for firewood. Especially when you think of its main competition out west, is the cottonwood. The bark is full of tannins and is used to tan hide. The leaves are used to treat colds and stomachaches.

Latin: Arbutus menziesii
Grow Zone: 6-8
Growth Rate: 3-5ft
Height: 50-130ft
Nitrogen Fixer: No

PROs
Flowers
Firewood
Tropical evergreen
Fast growth

CONs
It only goes up to the freezing cold regions of zone 6

Choke Cherry

Chokecherry is a wild fruit tree that can be found all over the northern half of North America. In fact, it is one of the most consumed wild edibles around. That's because it's just a wild cherry tree. Like most cherries, the seed is toxic. The leaves and stems are also toxic. Luckily, we're not interested in the leaves, we're after the fruit. The reason why it's called chokecherry is because this cherry fruit is extremely astringent. So instead of eating this fruit raw, you boil it in water and a little bit of vinegar to make a juice. You then can add a ton of sugar to make a syrup or jam.

The tree is a small understory tree that likes to grow on the edge of forests. It can be found in all of Canada and in all but 6 USA states. The berries when underripe are a bright red, and as they mature, they darken to a purple color.

Latin: Prunus virginiana
Grow Zone: 2-10
Growth Rate: 1-2ft
Height: 30ft
Nitrogen Fixer: No

PROs
Juice
Jam

CONs
Don't eat fresh
Everything but the fruit is toxic

Dawn Redwood

Larch is weird because it's a conifer that turns yellow in the fall and drops its needles. Dawn redwood is from China and was thought to be extinct until a strain was found alive in one Chinese valley. It's also a weirdo. It turns orange and drops its needles. It's also the cousin of the towering sequoias in America. This one doesn't get as big, but it can be grown in many more locations than its two picky cousins. It does have a lot in common though. It grows fast, loves water, and is rot resistant. Unfortunately, because it's only recently been plucked from near extinction, there isn't a lot of information on its timber value. Is it fantastic like the coastal redwood, or is it brittle and useless like the giant sequoia? I don't know, so for now, it's just a really pretty tree… that is edible and is used as a fodder crop for animals.

Latin: Metasequoia glyptostroboides
Grow Zone: 4-8
Growth Rate: 2-5ft
Height: 50-160ft
Nitrogen Fixer: No

PROs
Edible
Livestock Fodder
Pretty red needles

CONs
Not enough info on this tree

Hemlock

This is the most shade tolerant tree in North America, possibly the world. It loves the shade so much that it won't sprout if it's hot and sunny. Hemlocks like damp, rocky, shaded terrain. They're often found at the base of cliffs and along river banks, but they can also be found chilling in the shade of a heavy canopy.

Historically, the main appeal of this tree was the high tannin content in its bark. People would skin the tree alive and use the bark for tanning. The wood isn't bad lumber. It can be used for building things, but it's mostly used for pulp. The inner bark is edible and is a staple for survivalists. The fresh spring needles are also eaten. Medicinally, think of this tree as a first aid kit. The outer bark was used in a tea to treat bleeding. Once the wound is washed, the sap can be used to protect it.

Unfortunately, the hemlock trees are having some trouble in their southern ranges. Unfortunately, yet another pest hitched a ride from China is killing them. The bugs can't handle the extreme cold, so they're not an extinction level threat, but the hemlock trees are in some serious trouble.

Latin: Tsuga
Grow Zone: 3-8
Growth Rate: 1-2ft
Height: 40-160ft
Nitrogen Fixer: No

PROs
Loves shade
High in tannins
Edible
First aid

CONs
Southern range in trouble

CHAPTER 14
ORNAMENTAL TREES

So, this is the last chapter. Some people might say that a chapter on ornamental trees shouldn't go in a book on useful trees. Don't neglect the importance of pretty. Beautiful scenery makes the heart happy. Flower gardens exist to bring smiles. Pretty trees do the same thing. Sure, if you only have room for a handful of trees, plant the MORE useful ones. That said, there are tons of ornamental trees that were included in other chapters. Those trees are useful and happen to be pretty. These trees are pretty and might have some uses. Some examples of super useful ornamentals would be honey locust, mimosa, red bud, maple, sumac, sassafras, ginkgo, and so many more.

Cherry Blossum

Cherry fruit trees and cherry blossom trees aren't cousins, they're siblings. The two cherry trees are the exact same trees. We have bred and encouraged cherry fruit trees to put all their efforts into producing fruit. We did the exact same thing to cherry blossom trees, but encouraged them to put everything into the flowers.

You can use a cherry blossom to cross-pollinate a cherry tree, which is pretty cool. You can also use the cut limbs for smoking meat. You can even graft one type of tree onto the other. Cherry blossoms have magnificent pink or white flowers in the spring.

Latin: Prunus serrulata
Grow Zone: 5-8
Growth Rate: 1-2ft
Height: 15-40ft
Nitrogen Fixer: No

PROs
Flowers
Pollination

Crab Apple

Just like the cherry blossom tree, the ornamental crab apple, or flowering apple, is an apple tree that we have bred to focus on its flowers. The nice thing about crab apples is that they can go a lot further north compared to cherry blossoms. Due to how long of a flowering season they have, apple orchards often use crab apples as pollinators. This is why if you plant the seeds of an apple, the apple tree you get probably won't produce tasty fruit. Those seeds are 50% tasty and 50% crab.

Latin: Malus
Grow Zone: 4-8
Growth Rate: 1-2ft
Height: 15-20ft
Nitrogen Fixer: No

PROs
Flowers
Polination

Southern Magnolia

So, there's many types of magnolias in the world but I want to focus on my two favorites. This section covers southern magnolia, and the next one covers Asian magnolia. I grew up with a southern magnolia at a friend's house, and it was always my sisters' favorite tree. My older sister even bought one and planted it in my parents' yard.

Southern magnolia has rich, glossy, evergreen leaves. It produces big white flowers during the summer, and I mean big. You can use the leaves and flowers as a seasoning—they have a very strong taste. You can use the leaves like a bay leaf. A bay leaf has very little flavor, magnolia has a strong flavor, so don't use a ton. The flowers have a very sweet, lemony, floral taste and can be added to salads. For medicinal uses read the next section.

Latin: Magnolia grandiflora
Grow Zone: 6-10
Growth Rate: 1-2ft
Height: 60-80ft
Nitrogen Fixer: No

PROs
Big flowers
Pretty leaves
Seasoning

Asian Magnolia

I grew up with southern magnolias but the first time I encountered a saucer magnolia was at an LDS temple in Logan, Utah. Saucer is one of the deciduous Asian magnolias that can grow in much cooler climates. Logan is a fairly cold region, and it has long, gloomy winters. One of the cool things about Asian magnolias is that the flowers actually bloom before the leaves. So, you get these big beautiful pink and white flowers with nothing to hide them, right at the start of spring. It quickly became one of my favorite trees. Magnolias have been used for a long time in Chinese medicine. They're used to treat anxiety, respiratory, menstrual cramps, gingivitis, and to improve the kidney.

Latin: Magnolia
Grow Zone: 4-9
Growth Rate: 1-2ft
Height: 20-30ft
Nitrogen Fixer: No

PROs
Early spring flowers
Medicinal

Crape Mrytle

Crape myrtle is a summertime flowering tree. I've heard someone describe it as the unicorn tree because it has flowers that stick up in a cone and come in all sorts of colors. Pink, purple white, red...in all shades. You can get a dark, rich, red, or even a lighter color.

The thing I like about crape myrtle is it's a sacrificial tree. In general, a lot of your garden pests think your garden crops are delicious. This is where predatory insects come in handy. They think those garden pests are delicious. But what happens when they eat everything? They leave! Luckily there's a type of aphid, called the crape myrtle aphid...they think crape myrtle leaves are delicious. They will be so busy eating your crape myrtle that they will leave your garden plants alone, but they will also provide a snack for your predators. This keeps the predatory insects around while they wait for more aphids to attack your garden.

Latin: Lagerstroemia indica
Grow Zone: 7-10
Growth Rate: 3-5ft
Height: 20-30ft
Nitrogen Fixer: No

PROs
Summer flowers
Predatory in insects

Flowering Dogwood

The Oklahoma redbud is the only native ornamental to the US that is more popular than the flowering dogwood. Dogwoods produce these little white flowers. Now, personally I never was a huge fan of dogwoods, but when I bought my land, I discovered that I had a bunch and have no intention of cutting them down.

The bark has been used to stop bleeding and to treat colds. Dogwoods are extremely shade tolerant and like to grow on slopes, which is something I like because that's uncommon for flowering trees. The tree is small, but the wood is extremely hard & can be used for small things.

Latin: Cornus florida
Grow Zone: 5-9
Growth Rate: 1-2ft
Height: 20-40ft
Nitrogen Fixer: No

PROs
Flowers
Shade tolerant

Fringe Tree

There are both American and Chinese fringe trees. They're very similar and both are beautiful. Fringe tree is described as intoxicatingly fragrant. I'm pretty sure that means it smells really good. When in bloom, it puts on quite the show. It has these long dangly flowers, which is how it got its nickname, old man's beard. If the tree is female, those flowers will turn into fruit, similar to an olive. They are related, and fringe tree fruit is edible, but not desirable. In the fall, its leaves turn a nice light yellow. Medicinally, fringe tree bark has been used to treat skin irritation and to treat the gallbladder.

Latin: Chionanthus
Grow Zone: 3-9
Growth Rate: 1ft
Height: 20ft
Nitrogen Fixer: No

PROs
Flowers
Fall colors

Chaste Tree

Also known as vitex, it's a pretty, shrubby tree. It grows in warmer climates, so you will see it all over the southern United States. However, it is a fairly drought tolerant tree, so in places like St. George, Utah, this tree is in almost every yard. It has these little cones of blue flowers that stick up. While technically a nitrogen fixer, from what I can tell it's never used that way, so it's probably not a very effective one.

Latin: Vitex agnus-castus
Grow Zone: 6-9
Growth Rate: 1-2ft
Height: 10-15ft
Nitrogen Fixer: Yes

PROs
Flowers
Drought tolerance

Jacaranda

Purple flowers. Need I say more? This is one of the most beautiful tropical trees. Period. There is a reason it's been planted virtually anywhere where there isn't winter. It's a messy tree, so don't plant it somewhere you would like to keep free of tree litter, and yes, it is a mild nitrogen fixer.

Latin: Jacaranda mimosifolia
Grow Zone: 9-11
Growth Rate: 6-9ft
Height: 25-40ft
Nitrogen Fixer: Yes

PROs
Purple flowers
Nitrogen fixer

Royal Poinciana

Also known as the flame tree. This is also a popular tropical leguminous tree. Jacaranda has purple colors, but the flame tree has bright orange and red flowers. From the island of Madagascar, these trees grow fast and can handle drought pretty well. They love to grow big and wide, and produce a ton of flowers. The roots are shallow and are known to damage sidewalks and foundations. Oh and yes, it also is a nitrogen fixer, and probably a decent one, judging by its rapid growth.

Latin: Delonix regia
Grow Zone: 10-11
Growth Rate: 2-5ft
Height: 30-40ft
Nitrogen Fixer: Yes

PROs
Red flowers
Nitrogen fixer

CONs
Shallow roots

Lilac

Lilac is a shrub that is planted all over because it has so many flowers. Honestly, it's more of a bush than a tree, but it's a very big bush, and it's one of the most planted ornamental shrubs in the world, so I went ahead and included it. Lilacs produce these big clumps of purplish flowers. Some are light purple, some are dark. Some have more red hints, others more blue. Then there's a few that are even white. Lilacs are so easy to grow. They thrive off of neglect. They live for a hundred years, and can be found in the "wild" where old farms used to be. Lastly, they like sharp, cold winters, so if your climate is too warm, they won't do as well.

Latin: Syringa
Grow Zone: 3-7
Growth Rate: ft
Height: 8-10ft
Nitrogen Fixer: No

PROs
Flowers
Neglectable

Red Buckeye

Hummingbirds love this tree. In the spring it produces a bunch of little red flowers. Eventually, those flowers will turn into buckeye nuts. The Ohio buckeye is its cousin, and that's where Ohioans get their name. Buckeyes are so full of saponins that you don't want to eat them, but you can use them to make laundry soap. The tree is an understory tree and is very shade tolerant.

Latin: Aesculus pavia
Grow Zone: 4-8
Growth Rate: ft
Height: 10-30ft
Nitrogen Fixer: No

PROs
Red flowers
Hummingbirds
Soap

Orchid Tree

As you might guess by the name, it's a tree that produces large orchid-like flowers. The vast majority of orchid trees are from China, but a few are from Texas. The flowers are pink or white, and bloom early in the spring. It's an evergreen tree, all the way up until spring. At the start of spring, it will drop its old leaves and produce new ones. Lastly, the flower buds have been used in curry.

Latin: Bauhinia variegata
Grow Zone: 9-11
Growth Rate: 1-2ft
Height: 20-40ft
Nitrogen Fixer: No

PROs
Orchid flowers
Evergreen

Japanese Pagoda Tree

Not to be confused with the pagoda dogwood, this tree actually isn't even from Japan. It's a Chinese tree, but Japan is where English speakers were first introduced to it. This is a more obscure tree, but it is a popular ornamental. It has flowers in the late summer (a useful time slot for bees) and they form in pretty white clusters. Those flowers will very quickly form into little seed pods. Unfortunately, they're not a good source of food because they are mildly toxic. That said, birds like them, and the pagoda tree is considered one of the 50 fundamental herbs in Chinese medicine. I'm not an expert on Chinese medicine, but I would say if it made it onto that list, it probably is useful. This is considered to be a drought tolerant tree. Unfortunately, it doesn't like shade and even though it's a bean plant, it is not a nitrogen fixer.

Latin: Sophora japonica
Grow Zone: 4-8
Growth Rate: 2-3ft
Height: 30-50ft
Nitrogen Fixer: No

PROs
Medicinal
Late summer flowers

CONs
No shade
Not a nitrogen fixer

Camellia

This shrub can be as big as a tree, but it's always pruned to be a hedge or a bush. Camellia japonica will produce flowers in the freaking winter! Camellia, also known as the winter rose, is a subtropical evergreen that produces rose-like flowers in the winter time. Technically, different varieties of camellia will bloom at different times of the year, but I like the winter ones. Winter is boring.

Speaking of variety, the tea bush is another type of camellia. You know, the plant full of caffeine? The stuff people boil to make hot leaf juice? Camellia sinensis is the plant responsible for green tea, black tea, and sweet tea. Flowering camellias don't have caffeine, but you can still use their leaves to make a tea.

Latin: Camellia japonica
Grow Zone: 7-10
Growth Rate: 1ft
Height: 14ft
Nitrogen Fixer: No

PROs
Winter flowers
Evergreen

CONs
No caffeine

Ch1 Favorite
Black Locust
Empress Paulownia
Mulberry
Black Walnut
Willow
Sea Berry
Redbud
American Chestnut
Mimosa
Red Maple

Ch2 Fruit
Apple
Pear
Asian Pear
Quince
Pomegranate
Peach
Nectarines
Apricot
Cherry
Plum
Saskatoon
Sumac
Autumn Olive
Persimmon
Pawpaw
Jujube

Ch3 Nuts
Oak
Hazelnut
Almond
Chestnut
Chinquapin
Walnut
Pecan
Butternut
Heartnut
Beech

Ch4 Wood
Hickory
Osage Orange
Red Cedar
Live Oak
Ironwood
Black Cherry
Cottonwood
Redwood
Tulip

Ch5 Utility
Pine
Aspen
Sassafras
Yaupon Holly
Birch
mastic

Ch6 Nitrogen
Honey Locust
Alder
Kent. Coffee
Russian Olive
Golden Chain
catalpa
Goumi
Bayberry
Buffalo Berry

Ch7 Medical	Ch8 Trop. Fruit	Ch9 Trop. Nuts
Ginkgo	Citrus	Cacao
Elderberry	Loquat	Coconut
Elm	Fig	Cashew
Toothache	Banana	Macadamia
Clove	Tamarind	Breadnut
Linden	Avocado	Candlenut
Frankincense	Dates	Pistachio
Myrrh	Mango	
tea tree	Papaya	
witch hazel	Guava	
Gilead	olive	
Cypress	Starfruit	
Arborvitae	Pineapple Guava	
spicebush	Lychee	
hawthorn	Longan	
	Rambutan	
	Mangosteen	
	tamarillo	
	Soursop	
	Jackfruit	
	Breadfruit	
	Jujube	

Ch10 T. Nitrogen
River Tamarind
Pigeon Pea
Ice-cream Bean
Madre
Koa
Golden Wattle
Blackwood
Tagasaste

Ch11 tropical
Miracle tree
Eucalyptus
Rubber
Bay
Allspice
Oil palm
Neem
Ylang Ylang
Lemon myrtle
Sapodilla
Sandalwood
Tamanu
Tung Nut
Spinach
Mahogany
Teak

Ch12 Desert
Mesquite
Palo Verde
Desert Ironwood
Argan
Curry Tree
Carob
Jamun
Jojoba

Ch13 Cold
Larch
Ash
Fir
Duglas
Poplar
Spruce
Madrone
chokecherry
Dawn Redwood
Hemlock

Ch14 Ornamental
Cherry
Apple
Southern M
Asian M
Crape myrtle
Dogwood
Fringe
Chaste tree
Jacaranda
Royal Poinciana
Lilac
Red Buckeye
Orchid
Pagoda
Camellia

ABOUT THE AUTHOR

My name is Nathan Dickeson, and I hope you enjoyed this book. My goal is to help everyone to become more self-sufficient and a book on useful trees is just my first attempt. If you watch my videos, you'll already know this, but I am developing a fully self-sufficient home design called The Zion Home. The goal is to make an affordable off-grid home that anyone can build.
Stay tuned for more info.

If you see any grammatical errors in this book, please feel free to message me on in insta @nathandickeson

Also, if you made it this far... please please please go leave a review. You know how much of a difference it makes.

Made in the USA
Monee, IL
04 December 2024